More
Jack's Stories
Inspirational Stories for the Soul

Jack Rogers

More Jack's Stories
Published by Yawn's Publishing
2555 Marietta Hwy, Ste 103
Canton, GA 30114
www.yawnspublishing.com

Library of Congress Control Number: 2021900913

ISBN13: 978-1-954617-02-5

Printed in the United States

All quoted scripture is taken from the King James Version.

Cover illustration by Debbie Byrd

Contents

Story 1 Saved for a Reason   1
Story 2 That's Pretty Dirt   4
Story 3 Locked Out   8
Story 4 "She is a Church Lady"   11
Story 5 "Don't Die with your Music still
     in You"   14
Story 6 Racism   17
Story 7 "Everything is going to be ALL RIGHT" 21
Story 8 Heroes   24
Story 9 Comforting Others   27
Story 10 My Black Book   30
Story 11 "You've got to Lose Weight"   33
Story 12 Friendship and Perseverance   36
Story 13 "Damn! Damn! Damn!"   39
Story 14 God is with Us   41
Story 15 The Forgotten Group   44
Story 16 Why I don't drink alcohol   48
Story 17 The Joe Story   51
Story 18 "Pill the Fews"   54
Story 19 Overcoming Fear   56
Story 20 The Sock Drawer   58
Story 21 Sand in your Pockets   61
Story 22 What is Heaven?   64
Story 23 "Walking" with God   66
Story 24 "That Chicken Learned
     a Valuable Lesson"   69
Story 25 The Only Thing They Will Remember 73
Story 26 Immunity   76
Story 27 "You don't have to tell everything"   79
Story 28 Low Expectations   81
Story 29 On-Line Communications with God   83

Story 30 Don't Assume   85
Story 31 The Snake   88
Story 32 Flowers are Temporary   90
Story 33 Re-calculating   92
Story 34 "Rogers' Don't Cheat, Lie or Steal"   94
Story 35 Prepare   96
Story 36 Parables   99
Story 37 My way   102
Story 38 A son's love for his mother   104
Story 39 Excuses   106
Story 40 You Cannot Outrun Yellow Jackets   109
Story 41 Be Kind   112
Story 42 Children of God   114
Story 43 It Made it Worthwhile   117
Story 44 Point of Diminishing Returns   120

Jack Rogers

Story One

Saved for a Reason

One Saturday, before lunch, my parents did something that they had never done before or after that. My father was a mechanic who worked on trucks, tractors, hay balers, etc. One of the men that he worked for had invited us to come up and swim in his pond. We did not have swimming pools in Fort Deposit in the late 1940s. My mother made some sandwiches and cake for a picnic. My father brought some tire innertubes to play with and swim on. I was four or five years old and had learned to swim about fifteen yards at the most. I threw the tube out about seven or eight yards and planned to swim to it. The lake must have been at least fifteen yards deep at that point. What happens when the splashing of water nears a floating tube? It floats farther from you. I became exhausted, panicked, and went under water. I went under a second time and my lungs filled with water. I started to go under water for a third and final time when my older brother saw what was happening and threw another tube to me. The tube hit at the only place that could have saved my life. Why did God save my life?

When I was sixteen and had just gotten my driver's license, my brother got a job in Evergreen for the summer working for the highway department. We would take him down about 4:30 a.m. each Monday and pick him up on Friday afternoon after work. I asked my best friend to ride with me. On the way home we started down a long hill. Being sixteen and very, very, very foolish, I decided to pass a car on a two-lane road halfway down the hill. I was going way too fast and when I pulled into the other lane to pass, I saw a car coming up the hill right in front of me. My car skidded sideways, so I let up on the brakes and straightened the car out before I repeated the same process again. When I let up on the brakes again and straightened the car out, I was only a few feet from the car in front of me. The rubber on my tires was burning and I left skid marks on the road, but we were safe. I learned something about myself during this nearly tragic event; it was that God had given me the ability to remain calm and in control during a crisis. This paid off later in life when I was coaching. However, I did have to go to the bathroom as soon as we arrived at the truck stop/restaurant at the bottom of the hill. The breakfast sure was good after that. I have carried the guilt with me for years. My best friend was an only child and if I had killed him his parents would have had no one. He later became one of the best, if not the best, oral surgeons (endodontist) in the state of Alabama. Why did the Lord save our lives?

I don't know the answer to that question. Was it because he wanted me to share my beliefs and faith to my students that I taught and coached? Was it because he wanted me to share my faith and beliefs with my teachers and parents that I worked with? Was it because he wanted me to teach Sunday School to children, adults, and senior adults? Was it because he wanted me to share my faith in these devotionals I am writing? I don't think any of these is the answer. The answer is that God is simply a merciful God. Not just to me, but to everyone.

Titus 3:5 says it best, *Not by works of righteousness which we have done, but according to his mercy he saved us, by the washing of regeneration, and renewing of the Holy Ghost.*

Are we not thankful we have a merciful God?

Story 2

That's Pretty Dirt

My wife and I were driving to Rome one morning for her doctor's appointment. Our youngest grand-daughter, Rachel, who was two or three years old at the time, was riding with us. After we passed Cart-ersville, there was a large hill that had been scraped bare, exposing nothing but Georgia red clay. All of a sudden, Rachel yelled out, "That's pretty dirt." Now if you can find beauty in Georgia red clay, you can find beauty in anything.

My wife and I were both born in families that had very little money, to say the least. We were both teachers and struggled financially our entire working career. As a result, we had never travelled more than a few hundred miles from home. After Sandra was diagnosed with MS, we retired and decided that if we were ever going to travel, we needed to do it soon.

The week after 9-11, we took off to Maine. The high-light of our trip was going to the top of Cadillac Mountain in Acadia National Park in Bar Harbor, Maine. There was a huge white cruise ship from Eng-land parked offshore among the inlets. It was a beau-tiful sunny day, and it was the prettiest site that we had ever experienced.

In 2013, my wife and I decided to take a car trip out west on the northern route. By driving our van we were able to enjoy the journey as well as the destina-tions. We loved seeing the rolling cornfields in Iowa and Nebraska. We were impressed by the Black Hills and the Badlands. Next, we saw Mt. Rushmore and then headed to Yellowstone National Park. We spent the night in West Yellowstone, and I ate my first "bison" burger (not as good as hamburger). We crossed the Grand Teton mountains and ventured to Jackson Hole, Wyoming and followed the Snake River.

Our favorite sites to visit were the National Parks in Utah. Our favorite was Zion, followed by Bryce Canyon and Arches National Parks. Next, we went to the north rim of the Grand Canyon. How impressive!

We then traveled to Colorado to Aspen. It was early October, and the landscape was alive with color.

In 2015, we decided to take another car trip to California on the southern route (even though Sandra was in a wheelchair by then). We toured the Petrified Forest in Arizona and then ventured to the south rim of the Grand Canyon. The south rim was much more expansive and impressive than the north rim. You could even follow the winding Colorado River. While we were watching a helicopter appeared down the side of the canyon. A visitor had fallen from one of the ledges into the canyon. One of the rangers at the north rim told us that an average of six to seven people die falling into the canyon each year. We headed next to Yosemite National Park, perhaps the most beautiful natural area in California. We spent the night in South Lake Tahoe, one of the most beautiful views in America.

We saw the Pacific Ocean for the first time and then took the Redwood Forest Scenic Drive. Next, we drove to San Francisco on the Golden Gate Bridge.

Leaving San Francisco, we headed back home through Reno, Nevada. We drove many miles of difficult mountain interstate through the infamous historic Donner Pass. The next day, we drove through twenty-five miles of salt flats before reaching the Great Salt Lake and Salt Lake City traveling seven-thousand miles in fifteen days. What an awesome trip. It was a trip of a lifetime for us. America is a beautiful country!!!

One thing that we have learned in our seventy-plus years of living is that we can find beauty in anything we see, whether it be Georgia red clay or the Utah National Parks. It depends on our attitude and appreciation of God's creation.

One of my favorite words is "Focus". What we focus on determines our attitude towards life and our state of mind. If we focus on the beauty of God's creation, how can we have a negative attitude? I decided years ago that I would not associate with negative people. Life is too short.

My wife and I have a saying on our refrigerator which states:

"You have a choice each and every day.

I CHOOSE to feel BLESSED.

I CHOOSE to feel GRATEFUL.

I CHOOSE to feel EXITED.

I CHOOSE to be THANKFUL.

I CHOOSE to be HAPPY."

God speaks often about beauty in the scriptures:

1 Peter 3:3-4

3 Whose adorning let it not be that outward adorning of plaiting the hair, and of wearing of gold, or of putting on of apparel; 4 But let it be the hidden man of the heart, in that which is not corruptible, even the ornament of a meek and quiet spirit, which is in the sight of God of great price.

Philippians 4:8

Finally, brethren, whatsoever things are true, whatsoever things are honest, whatsoever things are just, whatsoever things are pure, whatsoever things are lovely, whatsoever things are of good report; if there be any virtue, and if there be any praise, think on these things.

Ecclesiastes 3:11

He hath made everything beautiful in his time: also he hath set the world in their heart, so that no man can find out the work that God maketh from the beginning to the end.

We have a choice every day – to be HAPPY and BLESSED – or not. The choice is yours.

Prayer:

Our Father, help us to feel happiness and thankfulness each and every day in all that we do.

Amen

Story 3

Locked Out

Sometime around the year 2000, our youngest son, Jason, was spending Thanksgiving Day with us. We both enjoyed running and walking, so we decided to spend a large part of the day running a thirteen-mile trail on the beautiful Berry College campus. My wife, Sandra, was going to cook our turkey and cornbread dressing while we were gone. We returned three or four hours later to find Sandra still in her pajamas in our garage. Our washer and dryer were in the garage and she had gone there to wash a load of clothes while the cornbread dressing was baking. Unfortunately, she had locked herself out of the kitchen. She remembered that I had placed an extra key on a branch in the front yard. She looked there, but couldn't find it. I later discovered the wind had knocked the key off the branch, and it was hidden under the pine straw.

It was very cold that day and Sandra had kept herself warm by occasionally turning the dryer on and standing by its door. We were very lucky to find the cornbread dressing was very, very dry but not burned and it was the best dressing that I had ever eaten.

We have laughed about this story many times since then, but it reminds me of something much more serious. Many times we "lock" people out of our lives.

I personally know a grandmother who is estranged from her family because she did not approve of something that her daughter-in-law did years ago. Now she is "locked" out of her family completely and has deprived her grandchildren of having a loving relationship with their grandmother. What a shame. This could all be solved with a simple, "I'm sorry." The grandmother herself is the one who is hurt most by her estrangement from her family, but her stubbornness does not allow her to have a loving relationship with her family.

I, too, confess that I have been guilty of "locking" people out. On two sperate occasions I have made comment to my daughter-in-law that offended her, with reason. In both instances my estrangement lasted only a few days because I, luckily, have a son, Jeff, who is a peacemaker. Most problems continue because of a lack of communication and Jeff provided that line of communication. Now, we all know that we love each other and have one another's support, even though we know that we are all human and will have disagreements.

There are earthly examples of "locking" people out, but they pale in comparison to our "locking" God our of our lives. How do we lock God out of our lives? Is it by not following his commandments? Is it by not loving other people as ourselves? Is it by not loving Him? Is it by not praising Him? Is it not worshipping Him? Is it by not going to Him in prayer? Let's look at what the Bible says:

John 14:6

Jesus saith unto him, I am the way, the truth, and the life: no man cometh unto the Father, but by me.

John 10:9

I am the door: by me if any man enter in, he shall be saved, and shall go in and out, and find pasture.

Matthew 7:7

Ask, and it shall be given you; seek, and ye shall find; knock, and it shall be opened unto you:

Revelation 3:20

Behold, I stand at the door, and knock: if any man hear my voice, and open the door, I will come in to him, and will sup with him, and he with me.

Help us in all our future actions and deeds not to "lock" God out of our lives, but rather to open the door of love and grace.

Story 4

"She is a Church Lady."

Last week Nashville, TN was hit by a devastating tornado that killed at least twenty-four people. What a tragic event.

This reminded me of another tornado that hit Nashville some fifteen years ago. My son and daughter-in-law were on a trip and my wife and I were keeping our preschool granddaughters. We decided to take them to Nashville for a long weekend. On the first night that we were there, we were awakened by a tornado warning at 2:00 a.m. They quickly ushered us to the main level in a hallway. We were seated with our back to the wall exactly the way we taught our school kids to do in practice drills. The tornado did hit less than a half-mile from the hotel, but luckily the hotel was not hit.

While we were seated, a nice lady kept walking up and down the hallway reassuring the children that everything was going to be all right. She spoke in a calm, quiet voice. When the lady passed, our youngest granddaughter said, "She is a church lady."

I gained two perspectives from her statement. First, Rachel had learned in Sunday School and church how a Christian or person of God should act. Secondly, the lady conducted herself in such a way that others would recognize that she was a person of God.

How should a person of God act? Like Jesus, of course! He set the perfect example for us to follow. Here is what the Bible says:

Ephesians 4:32

Be kind to one another, tenderhearted, forgiving one another, as God in Christ forgave you.

Hebrews 13:5

Let your conversation be without covetousness; and be content with such things as ye have: for he hath said, I will never leave thee, nor forsake thee.

Ephesians 4:26

Be ye angry, and sin not: let not the sun go down upon your wrath:

Luke 6:31

And as ye would that men should do to you, do ye also to them likewise.

1 Peter 5:8

Be sober, be vigilant; because your adversary the devil, as a roaring lion, walketh about, seeking whom he may devour:

Proverbs 15:1

A soft answer turneth away wrath: but grievous words stir up anger.

James 2:1

Jack Rogers

My brethren, have not the faith of our Lord Jesus Christ, the Lord of glory, with respect of persons.

1 John 1:9

If we confess our sins, he is faithful and just to forgive us our sins, and to cleanse us from all unrighteousness.

James 2:8

If ye fulfil the royal law according to the scripture, Thou shalt love thy neighbour as thyself, ye do well:

Colossians 3:9

Lie not one to another, seeing that ye have put off the old man with his deeds;

Philippians 4:8

Finally, brethren, whatsoever things are true, whatsoever things are honest, whatsoever things are just, whatsoever things are pure, whatsoever things are lovely, whatsoever things are of good report; if there be any virtue, and if there be any praise, think on these things.

Whether we are in a tornado, or just living our daily lives; others should be able to identify us as a Christian by our actions and the way we interact with others. Let us be examples.

Story 5

"Don't Die with your Music still in You"

(This story/devotional is written to all seniors and young people who plan to be seniors one day.)

I had the hardest-working parents in the world. They grew up during the depression and knew the value of hard work and money. My father was a mechanic at a local truck and tractor company. When he arrived home from work, he went straight to the garden and worked until dark. My mother was a stay-at-home mother raising her three sons. Later, she opened a small florist shop. The only times that she was busy was when there was a funeral, or a wedding in the small town (population 1454-1451 after my brothers and I went to college). Mama was a great cook and was always shelling beans and canning everything that could be canned.

My parents loved their children and would do anything for us, even though they were not hugging or touching people. I don't ever remember them telling us that they loved us, even though we knew that they did. They were not hovering parents and I don't remember them ever telling us, "No, you cannot do that or go there." That could be because they raised three PERFECT children.

We attended the local Methodist Church every time it opened and developed strong beliefs. They loved their grandchildren and spend a lot of time with them.

However, when they aged, they became more reclusive and during the winter would spend all day in the den watching TV with the space heater turned up very high. We would see them sitting side-by-side in recliners sometimes holding hands.

My mother developed Alzheimer's disease at age seventy-six and my father was a fulltime caregiver until he reached age eighty when we realized he also had Alzheimer's. We put both of them in a nursing home until their deaths.

I am now seventy-seven years old and my fear of developing Alzheimer's has made me more conscious of taking care of my body and mind. I exercise almost every day by either walking a five-mile trek up and down the hills in my neighborhood, working out at my fitness center on cold or rainy days, or playing golf on Tuesdays and Thursdays with the seniors.

I plan to keep my mind active by writing these story/devotionals as long as I can write. When these stories no longer make sense, you will know that I have developed dementia. Some of my friends say that time has already come.

What does the Bible say about aging?

Psalm 92:14

They shall still bring forth fruit in old age; they shall be fat and flourishing.

Isaiah 46:4

And even to your old age I am he; and even to hoar hairs will I carry you: I have made, and I will bear; even I will carry, and will deliver you.

Job 32:7

I said, Days should speak, and multitude of years should teach wisdom.

In 2001, a famous author wrote a book based on the most important principles that he wanted his children to live by.

One of his children has contemplated these ideas throughout her life, "Don't die with your music still in you." To her, it means that you don't allow yourself to live any life other than the one you were born to live.

Prayer:

Our Father,

Help us to not die with our music still in us. Help us to stay fresh and green. Thank you for sustaining us and carrying us when we are old and weak.

Amen

Jack Rogers

Story 6

Racism

We live in a world where racism exists. White racism, black racism, brown racism. Racism is not as bad as it was fifty to one-hundred years ago, but it still exists.

My father was a good person and a good father, but he was a racist. He was born in South Alabama in the late 1910s and grew up in an environment of racism. I remember when I was about four or five years old, he took me and my brothers to a KKK rally in the front of a local high school. The Grand Dragon of the KKK was present and spoke to the group. This happened in the late 1940s. I was very uncomfortable and scared to death. I did not sleep a wink that night.

I spent the majority of my thirty-four years in education working in minority schools. I was the first basketball coach in South Georgia to coach black basketball players in 1967-68. What an experience. I had a woman from a neighboring school threaten to throw a cup of hot coffee in my face. When we played road games, we had to have a police escort back to our bus after the game.

My conclusion after thirty-four years in education is that skin color does not determine the ability or possibility of future success. I can also conclude that the biggest predictor of future success of a child is whether they were raised by two parents: a mother and a father at home. I know that there are many exceptions, but this my personal conclusion.

When I was named the new principal at East Rome Junior High in 1989, my assistant principal was a black woman. She was the best assistant principal I ever had. We hit it off from day one. I could start a sentence and she could finish it, or she would start a sentence and I could finish it. We worked together as brother and sister for three years before the city voted to consolidate schools and we were assigned to different ones. One reason that we liked working together was that we shared a strong faith in our Lord and Savior, Jesus Christ.

One of my best bosses was a black Assistant Superintendent. He always conducted himself in the highest professional manner. We also shared a strong Christian faith.

What do the scriptures say about racism and prejudice?

James 2:8-9

8 If ye fulfil the royal law according to the scripture, Thou shalt love thy neighbour as thyself, ye do well: 9 But if ye have respect to persons, ye commit sin, and are convinced of the law as transgressors.

Galatians 3:28

There is neither Jew nor Greek, there is neither bond nor free, there is neither male nor female: for ye are all one in Christ Jesus.

John 7:24

Judge not according to the appearance but judge righteous judgment.

Romans 2:11

For there is no respect of persons with God.

John 13:34

A new commandment I give unto you, That ye love one another; as I have loved you, that ye also love one another.

James 2:9

But if ye have respect to persons, ye commit sin, and are convinced of the law as transgressors.

Proverbs 24:23

These things also belong to the wise. It is not good to have respect of persons in judgment.

Mark 12:31

And the second is like, namely this, Thou shalt love thy neighbour as thyself. There is none other commandment greater than these.

John 7:24

Judge not according to the appearance, but judge righteous judgment.

Romans 2:11

For there is no respect of persons with God.

To overcome racism and prejudice, there is <u>one secret</u>: we must stop seeing people of another race as a large group of peoples, but as individual creatures of God. EXAMPLE: I have stated that my father was a racist, but there is a lot of hypocrisy. When my mother started a part-time floral shop, she hired a black lady, who lived a couple of miles down our road, to iron clothes and cook occasionally. She quickly became a member of our extended family. We all loved her. Even after moving to Georgia to begin our work career; on holidays and long weekends when we made the long trip back to visit my parents in Fort Deposit, we would drive down to her house to visit and check on her. That is how much we loved her. We didn't see her as a class of people, but as an individual child of God. That is the solution to our overcoming our racism and prejudice.

Story 7

"Everything is going to be ALL RIGHT"

One of my favorite couples in the world was a retired Methodist minister and his wife. When our senior pastor at Rome United Methodist Church was reassigned to the Bishop's staff several years ago, he was asked to serve a long-term assignment at our church until the Bishop appointed new pastors in our conference. What a blessing for our church. In one of his sermons, he talked about going through some trials and tribulations when an old wise black man told him in a slow black dialect, "Everything is going to be all right." What a great attitude to have, and a great way to approach our own trials and tribulations.

I remember when my older brother died of pancreatic cancer in 2016, I had to remind myself, "Everything is going to be all right." My wife has had secondary progressive multiple sclerosis for the last twenty years and as it progresses, she becomes more confused and is losing her short-term memory. I have to remind myself, "Everything is going to be all right." My wife's nurse has suffered one major crisis after another with her health, her husband's health and tragic events involving her two sons. I try to remind her "Everything is going to be all right." Does it mean that God is going to take away our pain, our suffering, our losses, our physical illnesses, our tragedies, our crises, or any negative events in our lives? No, but it does mean that he is with us through these events, walking side by side with us and saying, "Everything is going to be all right."

Here are the Bible verses that comfort us:

Philippians 4:13

I can do all things through Christ which strengtheneth me.

Philippians 4:6-7

6 Be careful for nothing; but in every thing by prayer and supplication with thanksgiving let your requests be made known unto God. 7 And the peace of God, which passeth all understanding, shall keep your hearts and minds through Christ Jesus.

Matthew 6:34

Take therefore no thought for the morrow:

Isaiah 41:10

Fear thou not; for I am with thee:

Isaiah 40:31

But they that wait upon the Lord shall renew their strength; they shall mount up with wings as eagles; they shall run, and not be weary; and they shall walk, and not faint.

Romans 8:18

For I reckon that the sufferings of this present time are not worthy to be compared with the glory which shall be revealed in us.

1 Peter 5:7

Casting all your care upon him; for he careth for you.

Psalm 118:6

The Lord is on my side; I will not fear: what can man do unto me?

Deuteronomy 31:6

Be strong and of a good courage, fear not, nor be afraid of them: for the Lord thy God, he it is that doth go with thee; he will not fail thee, nor forsake thee.

I believe Philippians 4:6-7 holds the key to *Everything is going to be all right*. Paul says, *"let your request be made known to God."* Just as we can not be saved without first professing our faith in Jesus Christ, we will not be "all Right" without requesting God's comfort and support in our pain and suffering.

Story 8

Heroes

When we think of heroes, many of us think of sports heroes such as Tiger Woods in golf, Michael Jordan in basketball or Tom Brady in football. Many of us think of military service men and women, policemen or firefighters as heroes. Others think of doctors, nurses, and medical personnel as heroes.

However, most heroes are ordinary people like you and me. One of those is my wife's nurse who cares for her on Tuesdays and Thursdays when I play golf with the seniors. My wife has had multiple sclerosis for twenty years and is in a wheelchair. Her nurse's name is Wendy Clark.

Wendy's faith journey is one of being born into wealth and luxury, to being physically and sexually abused by family and extended family, to developing a major chronic lifetime illness (Lupus), to suffering one major family crisis after another, to finding fulfillment and peace in our Lord and Savior, Jesus Christ.

Her parents owned large houses (mansions), expensive cars, and lived a life of luxury. She drove a Mercedes convertible when she was a teenager. But there was a downside. Her father degraded her with oral abuse ("You're not worth the space you're standing on.") and he physically abused her. Her parents divorced and she was used as leverage between the two. Her father would tell her bad things about her mother and vice versa.

After graduating from nursing school (she worked three retail jobs to pay her way), her sister's husband used a date rape drug to rape her. She later lost the baby.

To escape her situation in New Orleans, she married a man from Greece who ran major floor shows all over the world. That was a mistake. He used her as a "trophy wife" and kept having many affairs with his other women. She could have tolerated this, but he began to beat her. One day, he bloodied her nose and pushed her down the stairs. She took her two boys and left with only their clothes and personal items. She left a large house and three expensive luxury cars, as well as diamonds and expensive jewelry.

Luckily, she met her husband, John, who loves her very much and is a dedicated Christian with great moral values. He loved her so much that he gave up a good job in Mobile as a shipbuilder, as well as his house, to be by her side during her long battle with Lupus, a chronic disease with no cure.

Anyone who knows her knows that her number one priority is her two boys. She often says, "DON'T MESS WITH MY BOYS!!!" She was determined to end her family tree cycle of physical abuse. Her proudest achievement is ending this cycle. Both of her boys are strong Christian young men with big hearts and caring souls. They work very hard and serve others, such as homeless people under bridges. They love their mother almost as much as she loves them.

During the last decade, she has suffered many crises. Her lupus took one of her lungs and required several surgeries to remove blood clots leaving scars on both arms. John had a major heart attack in 2014 and another one on May 31st of last year. He has not been given permission to go back to work. In the last several weeks her youngest son, Kamran, discovered a co-worker that committed suicide by hanging. He tried to revive him with CPR, but it was too late. Weeks later, his best friend was killed in a motorcycle accident. He has been devastated by these events.

So how does she get up every morning and go to work with a smile on her face? Her STRONG FAITH in Jesus Christ and never-ending support from her husband and two boys.

She has surrounded herself with Christian friends at church, at a youth group she serves, with a supportive Bible study group, and even with patients she works with.

She has learned that every morning she gets up, she has a choice to feel blessed, thankful, and happy; or she can feel sorry for herself. She chooses to be happy because she knows God is with her in everything she does. She is truly a blessed person with a supportive family and friends that love her.

Jack Rogers

Story 9

Comforting Others

I attended Lowndes County High School in Fort Deposit, Alabama for twelve years. It was a small school. I had eighteen students in my graduating class. The building was a U-shaped building with grades first thru sixth on one wing and seventh through twelfth on the other with the Principal's office and library in the middle. To say that our Principal ran a tight ship is gross understatement. The worst punishment a teacher could give any student was to send him to the hall because the Principal would look down the hall each period to catch anyone standing in the hall. The student's punishment would be a violent paddling or picking up trash during recess and lunch for several days. Even the teachers were afraid of him. One of my older brother's best friends once had to move a load of dirt from the baseball field to the football field. When he finished, The Principal made him move it back to the baseball field.

One of the students I went to school with was a dear friend of mine. My parents and her parents were best friends. Even though we were friends, we never dated more than three or four times. When Sandra and I got married in 1966, we moved to Georgia where we worked our entire educational career and still live there. My friend married a former roommate of mine at Troy University. They spent their career in

27

education in South Alabama. He ended his career as President of Troy University at the Dothan campus.

We went decades without seeing each other until I heard that she had pancreatic cancer and her treatments were not working. She lived about eighteen months after she was first diagnosed. I knew I had to contact her even though my brother and other classmates advised that they would not because they did not know what to say to her. I called her and that turned out to be one of the most fulfilling and rewarding things I have ever done. I called her every two or three weeks for several months before she died. We talked about our families, children, and grandchildren. We did not avoid the conversation about her ultimate outcome. I tried to tell her to take life one day at a time and to find one thing each day that she enjoyed doing.

My original purpose in calling her was to encourage her, brighten her day and give her something to look forward to. However, just the opposite of that happened. Her strength, her character, her faith encouraged me much more than I helped her. She was strong to the very end. She planned her funeral months in advance and asked me to speak. The First United Methodist Church in Dothan was packed. I wrote a good speech about her and made it to the last paragraph before I became emotional. My mother was a very emotional person and I inherited that from her.

I look back on those days and realize that when we try to comfort someone, we are the ones who are comforted most.

2 Corinthians 1:3 says, *Blessed be God, even the Father of our Lord Jesus Christ, the Father of mercies, and the God of all comfort.*

Let us never be afraid to call or contact someone who needs comforting, for Deuteronomy 31:8 says, *And the Lord, he it is that doth go before thee; he will be with thee, he will not fail thee, neither forsake thee: fear not, neither be dismayed.*

Story 10

My Black Book

My first principal's job was at East Rome Junior High in Rome, Georgia. My wife, Sandra, and I moved to Rome from LaGrange in the summer of 1989. My wife became the counselor at East Rome High School. This was the most challenging and the most rewarding years of my career. ERJH was seventy percent minority school which served two projects (East Rome and North Rome), as well as a large affluent white neighborhood. I had a great assistant principal and two outstanding secretaries. I also had an outstanding staff of teachers. Ninety-seven percent of our students were well-behaved, disciplined, and motivated. We did have our problems, however, any of you that have or have had middle school students know that at that age they are trying to find themselves. In faculty meetings, I used to tell our teachers that after spending twenty-two years at the high school level, I could assure them that their students would become real human beings again about the second semester of their ninth-grade year. Unfortunately, middle school teachers would never see their maturation. To complicate matters, there was a lot of friction between the East Rome and North Rome project areas. It manifested the week of the Rome City Fair at the fairgrounds. Many students would get into arguments at night that would carry over to the next day at school. That week I, along with my assistant principal, coach, and a teacher or two met at the buses as they arrived at school. Overall, though, it was a great little school with students being successful in many different careers.

One of the ways we coped with the stress of working with middle school aged kids was by using humor. I will admit that I have always been a bit of a practical joker. An example of that was each year, each school in the Rome city system would select a teacher of the year to represent their school. One year, I took a letter from our superintendent, made a copy, and then cut it off below the letterhead; made a copy of that and had our secretary type a fake letter to our teacher of the year inviting her to a luncheon honoring all "teachers of the year". The luncheon was to be held on April 25th at noon at "Joe's Garden" in East Rome. The trouble was "Joe's Garden" had closed a couple of years ago and was enclosed by a barbed wire fence with weeds growing knee high around it. I had someone forge our superintendent's name on the letter.

The trouble with being a practical joker is that you leave yourself open to being the victim of their practical jokes. I always told my staff that I kept a secret "black book" that contained the names of all those people that played jokes on me and that at some point when they least expected it there would be retribution. I never told my teachers there was no "real black book," but when the city of Rome voted to consolidate schools three years later and ERJH was dissolved, our staff held a final ERJH dinner to celebrate. My staff presented with a permanently sealed glass case enclosing my "black book".

Does God have a "black book" on each of us? NO – of course not! We do not get into Heaven by our works, but by the grace of God. In Ephesians 2:8-9 Paul says, *For by grace are ye saved through faith; and that not of yourselves: it is the gift of God: Not of works, lest any man should boast.* We will do good works if we are faithful to God, but that is not what will get us a ticket to Heaven.

In John 14:6, *Jesus saith unto him, 'I am the way, the truth, and the life: no man cometh unto the Father, but by me.'*

Thank goodness God does not keep a "black book" on me or you.

Story 11

"You've got to Lose Weight"

On October 28, 2019, I had my last six-month checkup with my family physician. When my family doctor retired in Rome, I needed a new doctor. My older brother was a patient of my new doctor and my brother highly recommended him. One Sunday afternoon, I was hitting golf balls on the driving range next to him and we were talking college football as we usually do. He is a huge University of Georgia fan, and of course, I attended the University of Alabama, a huge rival. I asked him if he would take me in as a new patient. He pretended to check his cell phone, and finally replied, "I've got one more slot for a University of Alabama fan, so call my office and make an appointment.

I had gone to have my lab work done one week earlier. During my visit, he said that my lab results were very good. He also said that I had gained five pounds since my last visit (219 pounds fully dressed).

He said, "If you gain five pounds each visit, you would be up twenty pounds in two years. At 6'1" you could lose five pounds in two days. Then came the dreaded words, "You've got to lose weight." I thought about his statement, "You could lose five pounds in two days." I thought to myself on the way to the car that I would wait until two days before my next visit and crash diet and lose those five pounds. I don't think that is what he meant.

I will have to admit that I am a sugarholic. I blame it on my father. He had to have a dessert after every meal, even breakfast. He could not sleep, so he would get up around two a.m. and drink a cup of coffee and eat a piece of pound cake. My mother was a great cook and she always had a cake or pie or both in the house.

All my life I have had peanut butter cookies or oatmeal raisin cookies in our house.

Just a few weeks ago, I decided that I was seventy-seven years old and now is the time to improve my health. My wife's nurse works with her two days a week and she made some strong suggestions, and she is just sneaky enough to check to see if I am following up on them. I have been avoiding sugar for a month and a half and I don't miss it. I am not having the highs and lows that I had previously. My daughter-in-law bought me a kettle and I drink a hot cup of water with a spoon full of honey in it every night before going to bed and first thing in the morning. I am a diet soft drink fanatic, and my wife's nurse is advising me to drink at two glasses of lemon water for every glass of diet soda. Unfortunately, it has not improved my looks, but I do feel better and I have lost about ten pounds.

What does the Bible say about taking care of our bodies as well as our souls?

1 Corinthians 10:31

Whether therefore ye eat, or drink, or whatsoever ye do, do all to the glory of God.

1 Corinthians 6:19-20

19 What? know ye not that your body is the temple of the Holy Ghost which is in you, which ye have of God, and ye are not your own? 20 For ye are bought with a price: therefore glorify God in your body, and in your spirit, which are God's.

1 Corinthians 3:17

If any man defile the temple of God, him shall God destroy; for the temple of God is holy, which temple ye are.

If we honor God and bring Him into our lives, we will change our eating habits. I have seventy-seven years of bad eating habits, and it will be hard for me to change. My mother was a great cook, but she fried everything in the 1940s and 50s. When I was teaching math all day and coaching in the afternoon and at night, I had to grab a fast-food hamburger when I could. My wife is a good cook and I always consumed enough for two or three people. Can I change my eating habits at this older age, or will I destroy the Temple of God? I guess time will tell.

Story 12

Friendship and Perseverance

When my soon-to-be best friend was named the new principal of Rome High School in the middle of the summer in the 1990s, he and his wife owned a house in Augusta, but had no place to live in Rome. Since our administrative workshop began the very next week. I called and offered to have he and his wife live with Sandra and me until they could find a place to live. Sandra was a counselor at his school, and we wanted to get to know them. We both liked to run for exercise, and this turned out to be the beginning of a long and close relationship. They lived with us for about two weeks, which allowed us to find out what a terrific young couple they were. Sandra and I were about fifteen years older than they were, and in the beginning many in town would see us out together and would ask me if he was my son.

This was not the first or last time Sandra and I opened our house to others who needed a place to live. In the 1970s, our best friends in LaGrange sold their house and were having a new home built for them. As is usual with construction their new house was not ready when they had to move out of their old house. We offered our house, and they lived with us a few weeks until they could move into their new home.

Jack Rogers

In the early 1990s, one of my former coaches at La-Grange High School was named the new head football coach at Rome High School and he lived with us for months until he found a place to live.

When my new best friend at Rome High School hired a new black assistant principal in the middle of the year, he lived with us for several days until he found another place to live. You really get to know a person when they live with you.

My best friend and I rode together many times to supervisor his athletic teams playing ball. On one of those trips, he confided that he and his wife were frustrated that they could not have children, even though they had spent thousands of dollars in an effort to do so.

A few years later they decided to adopt twin baby girls from China. What a brilliant decision. The twins are now sophomores in high school, and they have been the top academic students in every grade level. A year and a half after adopting the twins from China, they adopted a five-month-old boy from Guatemala to complete their family. Finally, a beautiful family.

My best friend became Assistant State School Superintendent for the state of Georgia and later was named Superintendent of Rome City Schools. When their parents aged and needed assistance, he retired, and they moved back to the Augusta area to take care of them.

My best friend and his wife are living examples of perseverance and what good can happen if you keep striving toward your goal and not give up in despair. They have a beautiful family to prove it.

What does the Bible say about perseverance?

Romans 5:3-5

And not only so, but we glory in tribulations also: knowing that tribulation worketh patience; And patience, experience; and experience, hope: And hope maketh not ashamed; because the love of God is shed abroad in our hearts by the Holy Ghost which is given unto us.

James 1:1-2

James, a servant of God and of the Lord Jesus Christ, to the twelve tribes which are scattered abroad, greeting. My brethren, count it all joy when ye fall into divers temptations.

Galatians 6:9

And let us not be weary in well doing: for in due season we shall reap, if we faint not.

My best friend and his wife remained steadfast under trial as James said in the scripture and in time reaped the harvest that Paul talked about in his letter to the Galatians. Now, because of God's grace and mercy they have a beautiful family.

Story 13

"Damn! Damn! Damn!"

One summer while my wife, Sandra, and I were working in LaGrange, Georgia in the late 1970s, we took a long weekend to visit her parents in Camden, Alabama. The new Millers Ferry Lock and Dam had recently been completed and we took our two young boys, Jeff and Jason, to see the dam. This was the first time they had seen a lock and dam and they were impressed to say the least. We walked across the top of the dam to the other side of the river and back.

We didn't think much about the trip until Sandra was walking down the hallway of our house, weeks later, when she heard our youngest son, Jason, about four-years-old, repeating the word, "Damn, Damn, Damn," one time after another behind a closed bathroom door. He was using different inflections and tones of voice. Sandra stopped, knocked on the door, and asked Jason what he was doing. His reply was, "I was just practicing." We don't know whether he learned the word from boys down the street or from our trip to the Millers Ferry Lock and Dam. Either way, we have gotten many laughs from telling his story through the years.

But is this not what we do- practicing sin over and over behind closed doors, or when others do not see us. What do biblical scriptures tell us about practicing sin?

James 4:17

Therefore to him that knoweth to do good, and doeth it not, to him it is sin.

1 John 3:9

Whosoever is born of God doth not commit sin; for his seed remaineth in him: and he cannot sin, because he is born of God.

Roman 7:15-19

For that which I do I allow not: for what I would, that do I not; but what I hate, that do I. If then I do that which I would not, I consent unto the law that it is good. Now then it is no more I that do it, but sin that dwelleth in me. For I know that in me (that is, in my flesh,) dwelleth no good thing: for to will is present with me; but how to perform that which is good I find not. For the good that I would I do not: but the evil which I would not, that I do.

I have spoken many times earlier in my devotionals that we have a choice every day – to keep on practicing and repeating sin, or to follow the will and example of Jesus Christ, our Savior. Let's choose to follow Jesus!

Jack Rogers

Story 14

God is with Us

Psalm 8:2 says, *Out of the mouth of babes and sucklings hast thou ordained strength because of thine enemies, that thou mightest still the enemy and the avenger.* This scripture was played out to near perfection by an event in my life today.

Let me set the stage for this event. This is Saturday, March 21, 2020, at the end of the first week of the coronavirus pandemic. The country is near a complete shutdown. People are sick. People are dying. People are working from home, if possible. All sporting events are cancelled. All public events with more than ten people are cancelled. The stock market has taken a nosedive, people are losing their jobs because the restaurants, bars and many businesses are closed. Schools are closed. Churches have closed except for on-line sermons. Our President and his medical team are holding daily press briefings before a hostile White House press core that would rather see America fail than our President succeed. Things are really bad at this point.

On Monday, I started having violent chills and my temperature spiked 101.7 degrees. I took pills for fever, put on a coat, wrapped a hot blanket around me an went to bed for the day. On Tuesday, I felt better and on Wednesday I awoke at 5 a.m., bathed and shaved and ran all over Canton trying to find

41

toilet tissue. I also went to my appointment with my foot doctor after I checked my temperature, and it was 97.8 degrees. By 3:00 p.m., however, my temperature was 100 degrees and I started having chills again. For the next forty-eight hours, I took two pills for fever every three hours. On Friday, I started feeling normal again and consistently ran a temperature of 97.6. On Saturday morning, I awoke at 5:30 a.m. and immediately began doing my Saturday morning chore of washing my sheets, dirty clothes, and sleep apnea equipment. At around 10:30 a.m., I went outside and saw a beautiful sunshiney day with a temperature of around 70 degrees. I knew I had to get some sunshine, fresh air, and exercise, so I put on my walking shoes and clothes and I headed out the door. With all the rain that we had been having, there were many walkers, joggers, bikers, and people walking their dogs. When I was about ¾ of a mile from home from my five-mile walk, I saw two approximately 7- or 8-year-old girls writing something all the way across their driveway near the road and sidewalk. They were using sidewalk chalk with bright, beautiful colors of yellow, pink, blue and purple. The lines and print, in large letters, were perfect and could be seen by everyone walking by. The words were:

God is with us

Wherever we go

God Loves Us

I could not believe two seven-year-olds girls had written this to cheer up all of the walkers passing by. That made my day and my week. Two seven- or eight-year-old girls were aware of the tragic events caused by the coronavirus and did what they could to cheer up people walking by and remind them that God is still in control. I could not wait to get home and write this story/devotional. Psalm 8:2 is right when the psalmist said, *Out of the mouth of babes and sucklings hast thou ordained strength because of thine enemies, that thou mightest still the enemy and the avenger.*

Thank goodness for children and parents who raise their children to follow the teachings of Jesus Christ our Savior.

Story 15

The Forgotten Group

This is perhaps the most important devotional story that I have ever written. This is Tuesday, March 24, 2020. We are right in the middle of the coronavirus pandemic. Everything is at a near lockdown. Schools are closed. Churches are closed. All sporting events are cancelled. Restaurants, bars, movie theaters, and all events with an attendance of more than ten are cancelled. Grocery store shelves are empty. Banks are closed to walk-in customers. Hospitals and emergency rooms are filled. Doctors and nurses are working long hours under extreme stress. Truck drivers are working long hours without a break.

This can be a very stressful time for everyone. We pray for older persons, like me, especially those of us with underlying medical conditions. We pray for the infants who have to depend on their parents to protect them.

But there is one group that I call the "forgotten group," that we should be concerned about. This is the group of young people ages seventeen to twenty-two. They are facing serious social, emotional, and mental problems. Many of them are seniors in high school or college and will never get to graduate with their friends or see them again. Many have lost their part-time jobs which they use to pay for school, their car, or their car insurance. They are depressed and worry about their future. Will they have a job when they graduate? Life is very uncertain for these young people. Let me give you two examples. First, my wife's nurse has an eighteen-year-old son who is a senior in high school. He has lost his part-time job which he uses to pay his car insurance. In his last three months, he has found a co-worker at his workplace that had committed suicide by hanging. Just a month later, he lost his best friend in a motorcycle accident. He is struggling and trying to find meaning in his life.

A second example is a bible study friend of mine who has a nephew that is graduating from college this spring with a degree in marketing. He is suffering from depression because he does not know what to do with his life. These two are examples of thousands of young people in this age group who are suffering at this time.

I have never been one to talk about a problem without offering a solution. That is just me. The Jack Rogers answer is four-fold. None of them are new, but I believe combining the four together is the best solution.

1. Exercise. I am a firm believer that daily exercise relieves stress, both physically and mentally. My wife has had multiple sclerosis for twenty years and is in a wheelchair. I try to exercise every day. I either walk a five-mile trek up and down the hills in my neighborhood, go to the fitness center on cold or rainy days, or pay golf with a senior group two days a week. I usually rest my seventy-seven-year-old

legs on Sunday. However, after church on Sunday, I usually find myself going to the driving range if the weather is pretty.

2. I am a great fan of a Christian financial advisor who has written many books and has a daily radio talk show. I have heard him give this advice many times. If you want to achieve a goal, help someone else achieve theirs. This could apply equally to this age group suffering from stress, anxiety, depression, and not having meaning in their lives. My advice is to find someone else who is having the same problems and help them through their struggles. It works every time. You will be the one who benefits the most.

3. Make and think about long-term goals. I am a great believer in goal setting. You have heard many, many times that suicide is a short-term answer to a long-term problem. Depression comes from only looking inward and not looking outward. Where do you want to be in ten years? Twenty years? Forty years? Life is a process that must be accomplished one small step at a time. When I graduated from college at age twenty-two, I was married, had no money, and did not have a job. But by the grace of God, my wife and I made it. Don't expect immediate results. I was forty-six years old when I got my first principal position. I discovered that was what I was best at and enjoyed the most.

4. My wife has a saying on our refrigerator which states: You have a choice each and every single day. I choose to feel blessed. I choose to feel grateful. I

choose to feel excited. I choose to feel thankful. I choose to be happy. The choice is ours to make.

This age group needs to know that they are not the only ones with these feelings of anxiety and depression. I was reminded of this a few Saturdays ago when my son, Jeff, took his oldest daughter, Ruth, and me to Kennesaw State University for a college visit. She graduates from high school this spring and has been accepted to Kennesaw for the fall quarter. She was very anxious, but Jeff kept reassuring her that every new freshman would share her anxiety and apprehension.

What does the Bible say?

Matthew – 6:34

Take therefore no thought for the morrow: for the morrow shall take thought for the things of itself. Sufficient unto the day is the evil thereof.

Joshua 1:9

Have not I commanded thee? Be strong and of a good courage; be not afraid, neither be thou dismayed: for the Lord thy God is with thee whithersoever thou goest.

If this advice is good enough for God to give, it is good enough for you and me to follow.

Story 16

Why I don't drink alcohol

Many people have asked me over the last decades why I don't drink alcohol. I guess my answer would be threefold.

1. I don't like the taste. That's the simple answer.

2. I have moderate OCD. I like to be in control of what I say and do. With alcohol, I am afraid I would lose that control.

3. The third reason is the story of my uncle, my mother's brother-in-law. He was an alcoholic and his drinking destroyed his life. I remember spending the week with my aunt at their house in the country in East Alabama. My first cousin and a friend from Sandy Ridge, who later received a basketball scholarship to the University of Alabama were also visiting that week. My uncle worked in Florida during the week and only came home on weekends. I remember being awakened in the middle of the night that Friday with my aunt screaming at my uncle at the top of her lungs. He had spent his weekly paycheck on alcohol and brought nothing home for his family to eat that week except a ham. That memory is embedded in my mind just as if it happened yesterday. When she screamed at him and asked him what they were going to eat next week, his only answer was, "But baby, I brought you a ham."

Years later I remember my aunt bringing him to a family reunion in a station wagon with his skeletal body laying on a mattress in the back of the station wagon. I promised myself then that would never happen to me.

My freshman year at the University of Alabama I wanted to prove that I belonged there, so all I did was go to class, study in the library, eat and sleep. I did attend all the football and basketball games since I was so athletic in high school. I attained my goals in that I made the Dean's List and was initiated into Phi Beta Kappa, the freshman honor society. However, I paid a price. By the end of the year I was completely burned out and could not concentrate on my studies anymore.

My sophomore year I decided I needed to enjoy more social life, so I joined a fraternity. I quickly learned that I was the only one of eighty brothers who did not drink alcohol and party. One of the senior brothers decided that he would blackball me when the vote was taken at the end of my pledge semester. Two of the other brothers found out about this and the night of the vote took him to a bar, got drunk and missed the vote. I did turn out to be the quarterback of the fraternity football team and star third baseman of the softball team.

After two years, I knew I was going nowhere and was not happy, so I made a drastic change. I left the fraternity (even though I had many good friends there, changed my major from pre-med to math, and transferred to a smaller school, Troy University, nearer my home.

This turned out to be a good move for me. In two years at Troy: 1. I became president of the Wesley Foundation; 2. I became president of the Intra-faith religious council; 3. Chief Justice of the Student Judiciary Court; 4. Assistant Dorm Director which meant that I had my own private room and bathroom. Most importantly, I married my best friend, Sandra, whom I met at the Wesley Foundation. We have now been married for fifty-four years.

I still love the University of Alabama and those three years provided me with experiences that I will always remember and made me the person that I am today. My two years at Troy were more profitable and enabled me to move into my career.

The two things that were constant during those five years was my conviction not to drink alcohol and my faith in our Lord and Savior, Jesus Christ. I learned that God is with me in my valleys and peeks. He will never leave me. Thanks be to God. Praise him all the time.

Story 17

The Joe Story

On this Friday, March 27, 2020, I am saddened to know that my good friend, Joe, is lying on a bed at a rehabilitation center in Austell, Georgia. He is paralyzed from the neck down which resulted from a fall at home in which he hit the back of his head. Because of the coronavirus lockdown, his wife cannot even visit him.

Joe and I met on the golf course several years ago. We immediately became friends. We both loved America and wanted our country to remain as one of our former presidents said, "The beacon of hope and freedom in the world." We rode together to several senior golf tournaments in Northwest Georgia. On those trips, he told me his life story.

He was born in Czechoslovakia and lived there until he was twenty-one years old. His parents ran a corner grocery store. When the Russian army invaded the Czech Republic, they confiscated every privately owned business. One Sunday morning, they went down to their store to find it padlocked with a sign on it notifying people that it was now owned by the government. They were left with no income, no food, and no property. They were lucky their friends shared food with them.

Joe was twenty-one at the time when he left home with only the possessions that he could put in his backpack. He walked through the woods only at night to avoid the Russian army. When he heard them talking in a group, he would circle around them to avoid being captured. When he made it to the border, he crossed over at a point the guards were not patrolling. He immediately found his way to the American Embassy. He was lucky to find a young American girl from a suburb of Washington, D.C. working at the embassy. She helped him and told him that if he could make his way to D.C., he should call her parents and he could live with them for a while. He then flew to Paris and later to New York City. He worked several odd jobs until he could raise enough money to fly to Washington, D.C. and meet the embassy girl's parents. He worked and attended college until he received a degree in engineering. He worked for an engineering firm outside of Washington, D.C. until he retired and moved to our Bridge Mill Community in Canton, Georgia.

We shared similar values of hard work and what we could achieve in this great country. This is the land of opportunity for all who are willing to work hard. We are dismayed by liberals and most college professors that are fighting for socialism and government control of everything in our lives. A noted research firm did a survey of most colleges and universities in America a couple of years ago and their survey found that 70% of all college students believed that socialism and Marxism are a more effective form of government than capitalism. That is what is being brainwashed into our children at all levels of public schooling. What a shame!! I wish every one of these students, college professors and liberals could spend some time with Joe to find out what socialism really is. Joe is not only a friend of mine who escaped a communist dictatorship in the Czech Republic, but my hero for doing so.

Galatians 5:1 says, *For freedom Christ has set us free; stand firm therefore, and do not submit again to a yoke of slavery.* If I have offended anyone with this story, I do not apologize.

I am not worried about the long-term fate of my friend, Joe, because as a famous talk show host said on his radio program every day, "Now here is the rest of the story". Joe was not a religious person until a few years after he moved to the Bridge Mill Community. He and his wife joined a local country church and he because a born-again Christian. I have read many of his emails since then in which he has publicly expressed his strong Christian faith in our Lord and Savior, Jesus Christ. I have faith now that whatever happens with Joe in his immediate future, Jesus will be walking beside him.

P.S. I found out two days after writing this story that Joe had passed on from this earth to a place of eternal peace and tranquility. May God be with his soul.

Story 18

"Pill the Fews"

I grew up in a beautiful little Methodist church in Fort Deposit, Alabama. Our only social life centered around our school and church. I attended Sunday School and church services on Sunday morning and MYF Sunday evening.

I remember dedicating my life to Christ during a weekend youth revival in which the guest speaker was a star basketball and tennis player at Huntington College in Montgomery. His father was a Methodist preacher and he followed in his footsteps. He later founded a huge mega church in Montgomery.

Our small Methodist church, the Fort Deposit Methodist Church, was part of a district MYF group which included a much larger church in Greenville. The district MYF leadership usually came from Greenville, but to be fair, every few years they would allow the president to come from a smaller rural and unsophisticated church. My senior year happened to be that year, and they chose a shy and naive Jack Rogers. I was always very nervous when I spoke in front of the group, but I tried to hide it as much as I could.

During the fall, we held a weekend youth rally at the larger Greenville Methodist Church. I was in charge and on Friday night I was trying to encourage everyone to come back and bring a guest with them. I intended to say, "Let's fill the pews tomorrow night," but it came out, "Let's come back and pill the fews." I was embarrassed and everyone got a big laugh.

"Pill the Fews" – Isn't that what we usually do in the church? In every church you will find that 20% of the people do 80% of the work. How do we solve the problem?

I tried to solve the problem as principal by identifying people whom I thought had potential and asked them to take a leadership position even though they were hesitant and did not necessarily desire to move beyond their comfort zone. I remember asking a minority third grade teacher to represent our school on a systemwide committee. She was very hesitant at first, but when I expressed my confidence in her, she agreed to do it and did a super job representing our school. All she needed was my expressed confidence in her.

To grow the church, instead of overloading the same 20% every year, maybe we need to identify others with potential and ask them to take leadership roles in the church. Maybe we could grow the 20% to 30%, or maybe 40% or 50%.

Ephesians 4:11-12 says, *And he gave some, apostles; and some, prophets; and some, evangelists; and some, pastors and teachers; For the perfecting of the saints, for the work of the ministry, for the edifying of the body of Christ.* In his letter to the Ephesian church, Paul is telling the people to equip all for the work of ministry, not just the faithful 20%.

disoriented that I could not walk straight for two days. I wanted to kiss the ground.

I decided to overcome my fear of heights by taking it head-on. My wife and I drove to downtown Atlanta one Saturday morning to a large hotel that has two outside glass elevators that you can ride up seventy-four floors to the restaurant and bar. My wife enjoyed the breathtaking views while I hugged the wall. I could not have eaten anything at the restaurant if I had wanted to.

That was a failed experiment for me as I still have a tremendous fear of heights at age seventy-seven. I guess I will have to close my eyes on my trip to Heaven, or the Lord may send me in the other direction.

God actually commands us not to fear or worry. The phrase "fear not" appears at least eighty times in the Bible, most likely because He knows the enemy uses fear to limit our hope and decrease our victories.

Deuteronomy 31:8 says, *And the Lord, he it is that doth go before thee; he will be with thee, he will not fail thee, neither forsake thee: fear not, neither be dismayed.*

Isaiah 43:1 says, *Fear not: for I have redeemed thee, I have called thee by thy name; thou art mine.*

God tells us where our strength comes from in Psalms 18:2 *The Lord is my rock, my fortress and my deliverer.*

Story 20

The Sock Drawer

In the 1970s, my best friend in LaGrange was help-ing us move to a new house when he suddenly started laughing hysterically. When my wife asked what he was laughing about, he replied, "The Sock Drawer". He had discovered my little secret. I have OCD (Obsessive Compulsive Disorder). My socks were neatly folded in stacks by color – black, blue, and brown. I'm glad he didn't see my underwear drawer. They are also stacked in order with the last one washed going on bottom and working up the stack to be worn next. That way they all wear out at the same time so that I can buy a new set.

When I take my change out of my pocket at night and place it on my dresser, I always place the coins heads up from largest to smallest. In my closet I al-ways place the hangers ¾" apart with the shirts color coded. I place my newly washed pants on the left, and it works its way to the right so that I know which pants I have worn lately. Years before my wife was diagnosed with multiple sclerosis, I had started to wash, dry, and fold my own clothes because I did not like the way she did it. Now, that she is in a wheel-chair, I do her clothes as well. Her shirts are hung with the last one she wore on the right and it works its way back to the left. She can now tell which one she wore to the doctor's office or church last time.

Jack Rogers

People ask me if my OCD bothers me. My answer is always, "NO, I LOVE IT – IT ONLY DRIVES PEOPLE AROUND ME CRAZY."

Being OCD is one of the many flaws that I have, but the Bible tells us that God uses flawed people to bring hope to a flawed world.

Paul was given a thorn in the flesh, which was most likely a physical illness, but that did not disqualify him from his ministry.

Abraham slept with Hagar, a woman that was not his wife; lied about Sarah being his sister; yet the Bible tells us he is the father of our faith.

Moses had a speech problem and killed an Egyptian taskmaster, but God used Moses to lead two million Israelites out of Egypt and eventually into the Promised Land.

Noah was a drunk but built the ark that saved his family and animals of every kind from the flood.

King David is one of the most highly revered and important characters in the Bible, but he had a history of making mistakes. In fact, he broke half of the ten commandments. Those included murder, lying, adultery, coveting a neighbor's wife, and even stealing another man's wife.

A weak and fearful Peter denied Jesus three times before becoming the leader of the new Christian church.

More Jack's Stories

When God spoke to Jonah and commanded him to preach repentance to the city of Nineveh, Jonah refused and ran away from the Lord. When he was swallowed by a whale, he repented and went on to spread God's message to the Ninevites.

From these examples we see that God is more concerned about our willingness to follow him than our physical flaws. I'll bet God is laughing today about my behavior in satisfying my obsessive-compulsive disorder. I hope that He is not enjoying it too much.

Jack Rogers

Story 21

Sand in your Pockets

I was born and reared in a small town in South Alabama named Fort Deposit. As you might guess, Fort
Deposit was once a fort during the Civil War, and
guns and ammunition were deposited there. My
wife's favorite story about Fort Deposit is a true one.
She tells people that the whole county has only one
red light, and the green light has been shot out of it
for twenty years.

I am proud of my heritage, though. I was lucky to be
reared in a Christian home by hardworking, simple-
living parents who never cursed, smoked or drank
alcohol. They were regular churchgoers and brought
my two brothers and me up to be the same. The
small Methodist church we attended was, next to our
home, the center of our lives in that small town. The
family itself was first.

I believe the family is still the most important insti-
tution in our society. I have read that man's priorities should fall like this: God first, family second,
work third, and the church fourth. I agree with this
order of sequence. I was in education for thirty-four
years, and I believe that most of society's problems
can be traced back to the breakdown of the family
unit.

How do we make the family unit stronger in order to
preserve it? You've all heard of love triangles, haven't

you? I believe a love triangle is essential in a Christian marriage. Now before you get upset with me, let me explain. The love triangle that I mean has God at the top and the husband and wife on the bottom two corners. As both husband and wife move closer to God, they also move closer together. But, if one stays the same while the other moves closer to God, the couple do not get closer to each other. I know that this has been true for me in my marriage. My wife, Sandra, and I met in church and we celebrated our 54th wedding anniversary this year. God has blessed us with two fine sons, a great daughter-in-law, and two beautiful granddaughters.

I have always known that my happiest times, the times when I am most content in my life, have been when I have been closest to God and diligent in following His directions.

Sometimes it is difficult to follow God's direction. Sometimes, there are things that we would rather do than bend ourselves to God's will. The story is told of two Texas cowboys riding their horses across the plains late one afternoon. All of a sudden, out of the clear sky came a bolt of lightning. The cowboys jumped off their horses. Another bolt of lightning struck right beside them. They fell to their knees. A deep voice came out of the sky and said, "CAMP HERE TONIGHT, CAMP HERE TONIGHT, AND PUT SAND IN YOUR POCKETS." The cowboys were too afraid to disobey, so they reluctantly put some sand in their pockets, made camp, and tried to sleep. The next morning, they awoke to find their pockets filled with beautiful jewels – rubies, diamonds, pearls, and emeralds. They were amazed. One cowboy looked at the other and said, "You know, I'm glad, but I'm sad too." His friend said, "How in the world can you be sad?" The first cowboy said, "I'm sad because I didn't put more sand in my pockets." We don't always understand God's purpose, but one thing is certain: when we obey Him and follow His direction, we are better off than ever before. The more sand we put in our pockets, in other words, the more disciplined we are to follow the Lord, the happier we are.

I also believe that a personal relationship with God must be a growing one that gets stronger with all of life's experiences. I believe that some of these experiences must be emotional and spiritual ones; just being good and doing the right thing does not make one a Christian. We all need to learn that the things of the world, the things that money can buy, cannot fill an empty spirit. We need to be emotionally and spiritually fulfilled. If we are not, we are like the young man who sent his girlfriend a diamond wrapped in a beautiful velvet box. When he called several days later to see how she liked her diamond, he found that she had not even opened the box. The box was so pretty she thought it was her gift. Without a personal relationship with God, we who call ourselves Christians are like the unopened box.

Story 22

What is Heaven?

It's exciting for me to be in a small Bible study group that meets every other Monday night. We do a very intense study of scripture and what it reveals to us. I believe this is a little sample of Heaven. This analogy was given to me by a friend on what he felt Heaven was going to be like. He said that as a small boy he was permitted to lick the bowl after his mother had mixed her cakes for baking. In considerable detail, he described the joy of licking that bowl and the immense pleasure he derived from the experience. When the cake was set on the table for serving, the rest of the family "felt" the cake was going to be a real treat. He pointed out, however, that he had lots more to go on than just "feelings". He had already had a sample. He knew that the cake was delicious. Then, my friend pointed out that the reason that he was so happy to know he was going to Heaven was that because through serving Christ on Earth, he had already gotten a "taste" of what Heaven was going to be like.

I'm absolutely certain that Heaven is going to be really wonderful. However, I love life, and I want to stick around on planet Earth as long as possible. Living a Christian life, according to information compiled from insurance companies, can help to improve life here on earth. According to their figures, the person who goes to church regularly will live 5.7 years longer than the non-church goer. That's interesting to me because so many people who do not go to church rationalize that Sunday is "the only day they have". Statistically speaking, if you dedicate Sunday to the Lord and go to church, He will give you the equivalent of forty extra years of Sunday here on Earth.

Proverbs 3:2 states this promise: *For length of days in long life and peace shall they add to thee.* In Proverbs 9:11 he repeats the promise, *For by Me thy days shall be multiplied and the years of thy life shall be increased.* This is verified repeatedly in the Scriptures. We also learn from insurance statistics that we as Christians have a 60% less chance of a heart attack and a 55% less chance of a one-car accident if we attend church regularly. God keeps his promises to us.

None of us know what Heaven is going to be like. Only God knows. All we can do is speculate. I think, for example, that Heaven will have the most beautiful golf course that I could imagine. If we don't' know what Heaven is going to be, then we should expend all our efforts and energy to enjoying Heaven here on Earth. We can do that by serving and worshipping Christ on Earth. That will give us a "taste" of what Heaven is going to be like.

Story 23

"Walking" with God

The last week of September 2019, my wife and I took my oldest son, his wife, and our two granddaughters to Seaside on Hilton Head Island for a week during their fall break. The weather was perfect all week. My son and daughter-in-law had reserved a four-bedroom house for us to share.

On Monday, Jeff and I played the Harbour Town Golf Course that the PGA Tour players play the week after The Masters Golf Tournament. I played above my head the front nine, shooting a forty, with a birdie on the nineth hole. The back nine was a different story. Holes thirteen through eighteen were difficult.

On Wednesday and Friday, we played two beautiful courses on the Seaside Resort. The golf was great, and the seafood dinners were delicious, but the most enjoyable part of the whole week was the three long two-three hour walks I took with my youngest grand-daughter, Rachel. The scenery was gorgeous, but the conversations I had with my fifteen-year-old grand-daughter were even better.

Sunday morning, we walked a couple of miles to the Harbour Town Marina and Yacht Club. We observed several beautiful yachts including a three story one that must have cost a couple of million dollars. We walked to the top if the Harbour Town Lighthouse and had a beautiful view of the boats coming and going out to the ocean. The shoreline was beautiful.

On Tuesday, we walked a couple of miles to the Seaside Beach Club. We walked up and down the beach and waded into the ocean. My son and daughter-in-law drove down to the beach club and were lying on the beach. We talked to them before getting a soft drink and walking back to the house.

On Friday, we took an even longer walk down to the south beach. While on the beach, we spent a long time talking to a man who was fly fishing with several reels anchored to the shore. He had some interesting tales that he related to us including catching some small sharks. By the time we walked up and down the south beach and bought a soft drink, I was so tired that I had Rachel call her mother to pick us up.

What's this story got to do with religions and worshipping God? It is a perfect story in that I have always felt closest to God when I have been "walking" with Him and conversing with Him. These are the happiest times of my life. People ask me why I enjoy my daily five-mile walks so much. I tell them this is my prayer time, my peace time, and my own personal time.

When you're walking with someone you're going to understand them better than you ever did. Walking with God is not just a time in the prayer closet. It's a lifestyle that we can only obtain through Jesus Christ.

Henry Ford said, "Those who walk with God, always reach their destination."

Deuteronomy 8:6 says, *Therefore thou shalt keep the commandments of the Lord thy God, to walk in his ways, and to fear him.*

Deuteronomy 5:33 says, *Ye shall walk in all the ways which the Lord your God hath commanded you, that ye may live, and that it may be well with you, and that ye may prolong your days in the land which ye shall possess.*

Jack Rogers

Story 24

"That Chicken Learned a Valuable Lesson"

When our youngest son was about five years old, we let him spend the week one summer with Sandra's sister who lived on a farm about ten miles from Union Springs, Alabama. We wanted him to ride horses and experience what country life was like. One day, Sandra's sister was going to cook fried chicken, so she sent Jason with his uncle to the chicken pen to kill a chicken. He did the same thing my brothers and I did when we were growing up. Uncle Keith cut the chicken's head off first. When he did, Jason observed a headless chicken running wildly around the yard for about sixty seconds before he fell to the ground. What Jason said next, we have laughed about for years. He said, "I guess that chicken learned a valuable lesson."

In my devotionals I have said many times that I grew up in a family that had very little money. In fact, until I was four or five years old, we lived in a three-room house that had no indoor plumbing or water. We took baths in a large tin tub which was filled with water drawn from our well. We used the bathroom in an outhouse in our backyard. The last time Sandra and I visited our old house the outhouse was still standing next to our old chicken pen. When my father and his uncle built a small three-bedroom house with indoor plumbing and "city" water, they

69

still used the well for drinking water and for washing clothes. They did not like the taste of the "city water". Every Monday and Thursday mornings before school, my brothers and I had to draw water from the well to fill the two tubs next to my mother's wringer washing machine. People born after the 1940s or early 1950s would not know what a wringer washing machine was.

When I was about ten years old, my friend who lived across the street and I were bored one day, and we decided to throw some loose boards down the well to hear the sound of the boards hitting the water. When my father found what we had done, he took me into the bathroom and gave me a good old fashioned "whooping" with his belt. Like the chicken, I "learned a valuable lesson".

My two brothers and I have always been very close. The three of us all loved golf and some of our most enjoyable times together were playing golf in a three-man scramble at my younger brother's small country club. The first few years we would always win money to cover our entry fee and more. As we aged, the younger guys could hit the ball so much farther than we could and we were not competitive, so we quit playing the tournament we loved so much.

Even though we were very close, my older brother and I used to fight a lot. I remember we were fighting in the kitchen one day and my mother could not break us up, so she called my father at work to come home. He worked about a mile from our house. Now that my brother has gone on to Heaven after fighting pancreatic cancer for seventeen months, I can confess that I started the fight by calling him "fat". He weighed about eighty pounds more than me. When we heard my father's truck pull into the driveway, I had mixed feelings. We had made our way under the table by then, and my brother was on top of me punching me as hard as he could. I knew my father would stop the fight, but I also knew what would come next. My father did not disappoint us. He gave both of us a good "whooping" with his belt. Again, like the chicken, I learned a valuable lesson.

There are many biblical characters who "learned a valuable lesson":

Peter denied Jesus three times, but he picked himself up and became the leader of the new Christian nation.

Moses was able to step up and lead even after giving excuse after excuse.

Joseph had a vision that kept him going in difficult times.

Abraham left his comfort zone to become the father of a great nation.

Noah did the right thing and built the ark.

Paul, as a Pharisee, opposed the spread of Christianity, but when Jesus appeared to him, he spread the message of Jesus throughout the known world.

Isaiah said, "Here I am, send me" when God asks, "Whom should I send as a prophet?"

Daniel's faith in God made him great even before he was thrown into the lion's den.

We, too, "can learn a valuable lesson" if we follow the examples in the Bible and follow God's plan for our lives.

Jack Rogers

Story 25

The Only Thing They Will Remember

My two brothers and I developed a passion for golf. Where that came from, I don't know. Neither of us ever saw a golf club or golf course until we went to college. In high school we all played football, basketball, and baseball. We were good athletes and loved sports.

For decades, my oldest brother was by far the better golfer He spent his entire career as a college math professor. He could teach classes in the morning and play golf in the afternoon. I used to kid him by saying, "If I didn't have to work for a living, I could be as good as you." He died of pancreatic cancer in 2016, and I really do miss him, and our golfing together more than I can express in words. I loved that brother very much.

When my wife was diagnosed with MS in 2000, we both retired from education and I started playing golf more seriously. By 2005, she could no longer climb the stairs to our master bedroom in our house in Rome. Since we were babysitting our two granddaughters four days a week in Canton, we decided to build a small cottage in a large subdivision where our oldest son and daughter-in-law lived with our granddaughters. We had the builder put in wide doorways for a wheelchair and handicapped showers. The subdivision has over three-thousand houses ranging in size from our small house to multi-million-dollar homes in three different areas. The subdivision has a beautiful golf course with a clubhouse and restaurant, a tennis clubhouse with many tennis courts, a three-acre swimming complex, a large fitness center, and a large playground area for children. Very nice!

After we moved to Canton, I took my first golf lesson at age sixty-two. My golf improved so much that by 2012, I was presented a large crystal vase for being the Most Improved Player at the end-of-the-year awards banquet. My oldest son and I won our flight in the Member-Member tournament several times. I won my flight in the club's Masters tournament in 2009 by shooting an even par 36 on the back nine on the final day. I also shot my age four times at the age of seventy-four.

Unfortunately, at age seventy-seven, my disabilities have caught up with me. I have a bad case of essential tremors and psoriatic arthritis in both of my hands that do not enable me to make a closed fist. I do take a self-injection shot each week which enables me to still play golf, but not at a competitive level. However, I still love golf.

About two years after Sandra and I moved to Canton, my older brother and his wife moved from Atlanta to a senior gated subdivision just northwest of Canton.

For a few years I played with him in his senior golf group every Tuesday. One of his best golf friends played with us several times. He was a much better golfer than either of us. He told us he owned and operated a Golf School Academy in South Florida. The Academy was focused on training corporate executives in the skill of golf, but also focused on how to treat their clients on the golf course. He told me one of the main points of interest was one I will never forget. He said, "Your playing partner will forget what kind of golfer you are, either good or bad; what your score was that day; but he will never forget what kind of person you are." That statement made a lasting impression on me.

How we treat other people will be how we are remembered. How should we treat other people?

John 15:12 - *This is my commandment, That ye love one another, as I have loved you.*

Ephesians 4:32 - *And be ye kind one to another, tenderhearted, forgiving one another, even as God for Christ's sake hath forgiven you.*

Romans 12:10 – *Be kindly affectioned one to another with brotherly love; in honour preferring one another.*

1 Peter 2:17 – *Honour all men. Love the brotherhood. Fear God. Honour the king.*

Matthew 6:14– *For if ye forgive men their trespasses, your heavenly Father will also forgive you:*

The biblical scriptures tell us how we should treat other people. Love one another, forgive one another, be kind to one another, and honour all men. If we do this, this is how we will be remembered.

Story 26

Immunity

Here we are in the middle of a shelter-in-place order from the government on Wednesday, April 29th, 2020. We have been told to stay at home because of the coronavirus pandemic. Everyone has been affected in one way or another, some are sick; some have died; some have lost their job; some have lost their income; and some are scared and have lost hope.

The problem is more than the virus itself. The problem is that we have not yet discovered a vaccine to give us immunity. My wife and I have taken the flu shot every year for the past forty years and for the most part, we have not been affected by the flu. We have both taken the pneumonia shots as well and have been lucky in that regard also.

Immunity is the key. How do we develop immunity? One of the greatest problems our country faces today is hatred and bitterness that exists between our two political parties. How do we develop immunity from hatred? I think I discovered the answer last night. I confess that I watch very few movies, but my wife's nurse brought us a movie yesterday, and we watched it last night. It was the best movie I have ever seen. It was a Christian movie. One of the three main characters cleaned out her closet and made a prayer room or "war room" out of it. She went to her war room every day and prayed intently to God. At times, she was even crying, screaming, and yelling for God to be with someone who had wronged her or been hateful to her. She prayed that the person would find God and change his sinful ways. She also prayed for herself. I will have to admit that I shed more than a few tears when I saw how God can transform lives.

I think that my wife's nurse wanted me to see the movie because she knows what a sinner I am. She knows by now that, among other things, I am very judgmental. I wish that I could say that having been a professing Christian all my life I would be less judgmental than I was thirty or forty years ago, but that is certainly not true for me. If I get to Heaven, it will be by God's grace and not by my works.

How do we develop immunity from bitterness and hatred? The greatest civil rights leader of all time said, "Darkness cannot drive out darkness, only light can do that. Hate cannot drive out hate, only love can do that." That profound statement probably came from biblical scripture found in 1 John 2:9-11; (9) Anyone who claims to be in the light but hates a brother or sister is still in the darkness. (10) Anyone who loves their brother and sister lives in the light, and there is nothing in them to make them stumble. (11) But anyone who hates a brother or sister is in the darkness and walks around in the darkness. They do not know where they are going, because the darkness has blinded them.

Proverbs 10:12 says, *Hatred stirreth up strifes: but love covereth all sins.*

Romans 12:9 says, *Let love be without dissimulation. Abhor that which is evil; cleave to that which is good.*

The Bible tells us how to treat our enemies and those who hate us in Luke 6:27-28.

27 But I say unto you which hear, Love your enemies, do good to them which hate you, 28 Bless them that curse you, and pray for them which despitefully use you.

Jesus tells us not to hate, but to love. That is the immunity we need.

Story 27

"You don't have to tell everything"

One of my best friends in LaGrange was my youngest son's elementary school principal. I went to college with him for two years at Troy University and we played on the same intramural basketball team. We were both members of a small Bible study group that met every Wednesday night for nine years. We alternated meeting at each member's house and our wives usually prepared us a light refreshment.

After Sandra and I moved to Rome to accept my first job as principal, we were told that he and his wife's youngest son had committed suicide in their backyard. It was devastating to everyone in LaGrange. He suffered from schizophrenia, depression, and drug abuse. My friend and his wife have honored his life by working with a movie company to make a movie named after him. Their purpose was to help other young people suffering from the same mental problems. Their dedication to this project represents the highest form of Christian discipleship. What a great thing they are doing!

When he was principal of my son's elementary school, my son's teacher sent Jason and a friend of his to the principal's office for talking when they were supposed to be having quiet time. When my friend asked them what they were doing wrong, Jason's friend opened up and told my friend everything they had done wrong for an extended period of time. Finally, Jason leaned over and whispered to his friend, "You don't have to tell him everything." I don't know how my friend could maintain his composure and not start laughing.

My friend and I played a lot of golf together through the years and my son's statement provided us a lot of lighthearted humor.

One thing we all know is we "don't have to tell" God everything because He already knows.

1 John 3:20 – *For if our heart condemn us, God is greater than our heart, and knoweth all things.*

Psalms 139:4 – *For there is not a word in my tongue, but, lo, O Lord, thou knowest it altogether.*

Hebrews 4:13 – *Neither is there any creature that is not manifest in his sight: but all things are naked and opened unto the eyes of him with whom we have to do.*

Even though God already knows everything, he still wants us to go to him in prayer. He wants us to praise him and thank him for our blessings; to ask him for forgiveness for our sins; and to come to him with our concerns for other people on our prayer list.

Story 28

Low Expectations

In 2013, Sandra and I took our first car trip out west (which I detailed at length in an earlier devotional). On our way home, after we left Arches National Park in Utah, we planned to drive directly to Aspen Village in Colorado. We intended to take 91 North, but I mistakenly took 91 South, plunging deep into the Navaho Indian Reservation. Our country did not treat the Indian Nation very well when we forced them out west into this barren wasteland. They live with a single power line leading to their homes. There were few trees and almost no grass anywhere. They mostly live off government benefits. It was a very depressing site. After about an hour and a half, we stopped at a hamburger joint to use the restroom. Every employee and customer there was Navajo. Sandra was in a wheelchair, and they were very courteous to us. We stopped at a gas station to get directions and found out we needed to backtrack one-hundred and five miles and go north to Colorado. By the time we left the Navaho Reservation, it was 4:00 p.m. and we had not had lunch. We finally found a restaurant, but there was only one car parked in front. It had a dirt parking lot with wooden stairs leading to a porch in front. There was only one customer inside and he left soon after we arrived. There was only one waitress and one cook. We had very low expectations about the quality of the food we would get, so we played it safe and each ordered a hamburger and fries. Boy, were we surprised when the food came. It was the best hamburger I have ever eaten in my seventy-seven years. I don't know what kind of bread the bun was, but it was delicious. We complimented the waitress and cook and left very full and happy.

Biblical scriptures tell us what God's expectations are:

Proverbs 10:28 – *The hope of the righteous shall be gladness; but the expectation of the wicked shall perish.*

Philippians 4:6 – *Be careful for nothing; but in every thing by prayer and supplication with thanksgiving let your requests be made known unto God.*

And the most important one of all:

Luke 12:40 – *Be ye therefore ready also: for the Son of man cometh at an hour when ye think not.*

God does not have low expectations of us, but expects us to live a life patterned after his son, Jesus Christ. He expects us to live a life of love and service to all. By doing that we be ready when the Son of Man does return.

Jack Rogers

Story 29

On-Line Communications with God

Today, (Friday, April 17th, 2020), during my daily five-mile walk, I stopped to talk with a golfing friend who teaches at a county high school. I asked him how the online teaching and learning was going. The schools are closed due to shelter-in-place orders from the governor during this worldwide pandemic. His answer was, "Online learning is not what it was promoted to be." There is no personal interaction between students and teachers. The teacher does not know his students have the technology to make it work. He does not know if the student's parents have lost their jobs during the recession. Does the student have enough food at home to eat? If the students' grades fall from an A to a C, will they lose their HOPE scholarship? If the stock market loses 25% of its value, will parents have enough money to send their children to college? Of course, the online education did not cause these problems, we know the coronavirus pandemic was the cause, but the result is still the same.

We know that prayer is the way we communicate with our Lord and Savior, but can we communicate online? In the 1970s, Sandra and I were in the same Sunday School class in LaGrange with our high school band director and his wife. One Sunday he made a statement that startled me. He said that since God knows everything already, he never talks personally with his God. He said God knows he loves him and worships him and knows his needs, so why communicate with him in prayer? I disagreed with him because I believe we should pray to God as often as possible.

What do biblical scriptures tell us about why we should pray?

1 John 5:14 – *And this is the confidence that we have in him, that, if we ask any thing according to his will, he heareth us:*

Philippians 4:6 – *Be careful for nothing; but in every thing by prayer and supplication with thanksgiving let your requests be made known unto God.*

1 Thessalonians 5:17 – *Pray without ceasing.*

Romans 12:12 – *Rejoicing in hope; patient in tribulation; continuing instant in prayer;*

Jeremiah 29:12 – *Then shall ye call upon me, and ye shall go and pray unto me, and I will hearken unto you.*

James 5:13 – *Is any among you afflicted? let him pray. Is any merry? let him sing psalms.*

The Bible is clear: we are to be faithful in prayer; ask anything according to his will; and he will listen to us.

So as Paul said to the Thessalonians –

Pray continually.

Story 30

Don't Assume

When my wife, Sandra, graduated from Troy University in 1967, I had just completed my first year of teaching math and coaching at a small high school in Coffee County, Alabama, just sixteen miles from Troy. Sandra was very smart and graduated in three years by going to school during the summer. She was editor of the college newspaper her senior year. It took me four terms to graduate (Kennedy, Johnson, Nixon and Carter).

When she graduated, we accepted an offer to teach and coach in Fitzgerald, Georgia. Even though we moved six hours away from our families, it turned out to be one of the best decisions of our lives. We loved the five years we worked in the South Georgia town of Fitzgerald. The story is that Fitzgerald was settled by a large number of "Damn Yankees" after the Civil War (or war of northern aggression against the South). When they came to fight, they fell in love with the weather, among other things, and moved their families to Fitzgerald. Fitzgerald was largely a farming community, raising crops such as tobacco, corn and cotton. You might say the people were God's people. They were hard working, friendly, and very supportive of their schools.

Like most South Georgia towns, football was king and Friday night was the social event of the week.

More Jack's Stories

We had good players and good teams. We only lost five regular season games in five years. My first year I coached the eighth-grade team and moved up with them to the ninth-grade team the next year. After practice one fall, I gathered my team together after wind sprints and was talking to them when they lifted me up on their shoulders and carried me to the back of the fieldhouse. Their parents had prepared a "baby shower" with refreshments for my wife, Sandra. That was the kind of people they were.

Since Sandra and I both worked long hours, most of our friends were schoolteachers. One Saturday night, we invited another young teaching couple over for dinner (or supper as we said in South Alabama in the 1950s). We always cooked our meats well done, so I did the same with the steaks. Sandra will not eat any meat with pink in it to this day.

When I served our well-done steaks, I noticed our male guest fiddled around with his, but never ate any. I thought that was odd, but I just justified it to myself that he was from Tennessee and might be a little odd. The middle of the next week, his wife confessed to Sandra that he only ate his steak rare.

His thought was that I had wasted his expensive steak by overcooking it. That proved to me that I shouldn't have "assumed" that other people like something just because I do. A lesson well learned.

Proverbs 3:7 says, *Be not wise in thine own eyes: fear the Lord, and depart from evil.*

Jack Rogers

Proverbs 18:13 says, *He that answereth a matter before he heareth it, it is folly and shame unto him.*

Proverbs 18:13 tells me personally that even in a small thing like cooking a steak, I should have heard how my guest wanted his steak cooked before I answered it myself. It was folly and brought shame on me.

Story 31

The Snake

In the late 1970s, when our youngest son, Jason, was about five years old, he developed a fascination with snakes. At the end of that school year, Sandra and I decided to take our boys to the Gulf Coast near Panama City, Florida for a few days before I began my summer job. As we neared Panama City, Jason spotted Snake-A-Torium on the side of the road. He insisted that we turn around and tour the Snake-A-Torium. We had his picture taken with a large python wrapped around his shoulders. We still have the picture. He was a proud boy.

I do not share Jason's love of snakes. In fact, I am scared of them. I probably inherited that from my mother. When my brothers and I were young, we built a small two-story hut behind our house with some scrap lumber. One morning, we entered the hut to find a large snake on the ground floor. We raced to tell our mother and she grabbed my father's 22 rifle. She probably killed the snake with her first shot, but she continued to shoot twenty-seven more times until the chamber was empty.

What is the most important snake story ever told? Of course, it is the story of Eve and the snake in Genesis, the first book of the Bible.

Adam was in the Garden of Eden when God told him that he was free to eat from any tree in the garden, but he must not eat from the tree of knowledge of good and evil, for if you eat from it you will surely die.

Now when the serpent approached Eve, he told her that she would not die, but that her eyes would be opened and she would be like God, knowing good from evil. She saw the fruit of the tree was good and pleasing to the eye, so she took some and ate it. She also gave some to Adam and he ate it. When confronted by God, Adam tried to blame it on Eve. She then said that the serpent had deceived her. God then put a curse on the serpent, so that he would have to crawl on his belly all the days of his life and eat dust.

One of Satan's greatest tricks is deceiving people into choosing sin by promising them something greater. Just as there was for Adam and Eve, there are always consequences for sin. We either hurt ourselves or someone we love. Adam and Eve fell from grace. Let us not choose sin.

Story 32

Flowers are Temporary

When my brothers and I were young, my mother opened a small floral shop next to our house in Fort Deposit, Alabama. Her first cousin financed the shop since we had very little money. The only time that my mother was busy was when we had a wedding or funeral in our small town. Other than those events, she only did occasional flowers for church decorations or high school proms and such. When she did the flowers for a well-known person in the community or county who died, she might work for thirty consecutive hours or more before the funeral. She worked very hard and our female neighbors would help.

My job was to drive the thirty miles to Montgomery to a wholesale flower shop to pick up fresh flowers for the blanket and sprays. On the day of the funeral, I would make a last-minute trip to the church to deliver and arrange the final flowers. Many of the funerals were in small churches in the rural county. The churches did not have air conditioning in the 1950s, so I would wait outside the church until the funeral was over. The windows were open, so I could hear the preacher pronounce the final prayer. When he did, I would run in the back of the church, grab the standing sprays and potted plants and load them into the back of our station wagon. I would rush them to the gravesite, trying to beat the mourners. My job did not end there. Three or four days later, I would go to the gravesite and collect the dead flowers. My mother recycled the styrofoam backs of the sprays, so I would go to the large ditch behind our house and pull the flowers out of the styrofoam backs. That was my least favorite part because my hands stayed cracked and bloody.

With apologies to my wife, because of my childhood experiences, I am not a fan of cut flowers in a vase in the house. They are pretty one day and then they wilt and dry up. However, I truly love outside flower gardens in the spring. They are beautiful.

There is one thing in life which will never dry up and wilt; that is the love of God.

Deuteronomy 31:8 – *And the Lord, he it is that doth go before thee; he will be with thee, he will not fail thee, neither forsake thee: fear not, neither be dismayed.*

Joshua 1:5 – *There shall not any man be able to stand before thee all the days of thy life: as I was with Moses, so I will be with thee: I will not fail thee, nor forsake thee.*

We know that God will not wilt or dry up. Remember, God will be with us always and forever.

Story 33

Re-calculating

My GPS device is a very handy tool. I wish I had owned one many years earlier. I grew up in rural South Alabama and I could easily get directions from anyone along the highway. The South has a reputation for friendliness and hospitality and that was true. I admit that I hate driving in a big city, especially Atlanta. Unfortunately, except for our first move, every time we moved it was closer to Atlanta. When Sandra graduated from Troy University in 1967, we accepted positions in Fitzgerald, the colony city, located in South Georgia, a parallel move. Five years later, we moved to the beautiful city of La-Grange just one and a half hours from Atlanta. After seventeen more years, I accepted a principal's position in Rome, just one hour from Atlanta. We still love Rome and have many friends there. When Sandra was diagnosed with MS, we had to downsize, so in 2005, we built a small cottage in the beautiful Bridge Mill Subdivision in Canton, Georgia. Canton is located in the outskirts of Atlanta, but we moved into the same subdivision as our oldest son, daughter-in-law, and two granddaughters. Sandra and I are very fortunate in that we truly loved every city we lived in. However, we both have decided that our next move will be to a nursing home or worse.

Many times, when I used my GPS, I still miss a turn if I am in the wrong lane. The GPS will say turn left in two miles. Then turn left in one mile. Then five-hundred yards. Then one-hundred yards. When I miss my left turn, the GPS will go silent for a minute and then say "re-calculating". Luckily, it does not say, "You idiot, I told you to turn left" or "Why didn't you do what I told you to do? I'm sure that is what you would hear from your spouse. No, the GPS gives you a second chance.

Second and third chances, isn't that what God gives us? We should rejoice in the fact that God gives multiple chances.

Some quotes about second chances include:

"When it comes to God, we can't run of second chances...only time."

"Every moment of your life is a second chance."

"If God gave you a second chance...don't waste it."

"You've never gone so far that God can't redeem you, restore you, forgive you, and give you a second chance."

God gave Jonah and Samson second chances. God does not keep a record of our sins so that when we reach a certain number, he will stop forgiving us. This isn't like baseball game when after three strikes you're out. God never gives up on us.

Story 34

"Rogers' Don't Cheat, Lie or Steal"

Our youngest son, Jason, was asked to write an essay about himself in a freshman English course at Georgia Tech. At the beginning of the course, the professor asked each student to tell him "who they were". Jason wrote his essay on "Rogers' don't cheat, lie or steal." I guess he had that ingrained in him from birth by his parents.

The negative aspect of having both parents that were teachers is that they know everything you do at school from Kindergarten through high school. I remember one afternoon Sandra picked Jason up from his kindergarten school after she left work at La-Grange High School. After leaving his school, they ran into a heavy hailstorm. Sandra parked her car in the street because she thought the ice was going to break the windshield. Unfortunately, that memory stayed with Jason for years. His teachers would catch him looking out the window worried about the weather and not focusing on his schoolwork. Jason was a C student at best through his elementary and junior high years. His junior high school counselor recommended putting him in lower-level classes at LaGrange High School. Sandra and I convinced him to put Jason in college prep classes and give him a chance to succeed. Suddenly, a light bulb came on and Jason's grades in ninth grade went from C's to A's. He made the National Honor Society and was admitted to Georgia Tech. He even received a small scholarship from the Georgia Coaches Association of which I was a member. The lesson here is never give up on a child. You never know when the light bulb is going to come on, as it did with Jason in his ninth grade year.

Jason's essay in college reminds me of how we should follow the ten commandments as stated in Exodus 20 in the Holy Bible. The statement, "Rogers' don't cheat, lie, or steal comes from the 8th, 9th and 10th commandments:

8. Do not steal.

9. Do not testify or bear false witness against your neighbor and,

10. Do not covet.

We should obey the commandments as given to Moses on Mount Sinai, obey the Bible, and be good people; however, we are not saved by obeying the ten commandments; we are saved by God's grace alone.

In the New Testament, Jason's essay was summed up in Mark 10:19 – *You know the commandments: Do not murder, Do not commit adultery, Do not steal, Do not bear false witness, Do not defraud, Honor your father and mother.*

These commandments apply to us today just as they did to the Israelites in the Old Testament. Jason's essay was right on.

Story 35

Prepare

Undoubtedly, water sports were never intended to be my cup of tea. Not that I didn't enjoy water sports, but one negative event after another led me to believe that golf should be my passion.

In story eight of my first book, "Traveling Without a Driver," I told the story of my friend falling out of a boat that he was driving while pulling a skier. Scary, but true story. In the first story of my second book, "Saved for a Reason," I told the story of coming within mere seconds of drowning in a private lake when I was four or five years old. Again, scary but true story.

Unfortunately, those were not the only negative events in my life involving water sports. In high school, my small class had a skiing party on a small lake on property owned by the father of a classmate. When it was my turn, the driver took me into a narrow inlet to turn around. When I made a wide turnaround of the boat, I ran out of the water into the grassy pasture. Being a totally inexperienced skier, I held on to the ski rope for about fifty yards until I entered the water again. Only the Lord kept me from hitting the small tree stubs in the pasture.

In the 1980s, my wife and I bought a small house in LaGrange. Since the house was less than five miles from West Point Lake, it was only logical to me to buy a used ski and fishing boat. When my parents came to Atlanta to spend the weekend with my older brother, we invited the whole family to picnic with us on the lake, and we would take turns riding my ski boat up and down the lake. In my excitement to show off my used ski boat, I failed to prepare properly. When my brother and I launched the boat and drove about five-hundred yards from shore, I realized that I had not prepared the boat before sliding it off the trailer. I had forgotten to put the plug in the drain hole in the rear of the boat. The boat was quickly filling up with water. Being a new boat owner, I didn't know what to do, so I drove the boat back to the boat ramp and loaded the boat on the trailer. Unfortunately, I didn't know the inexpensive trailer could not handle the weight of the boat when it was filled with water. It ruined our day on the lake, as well as forced me to buy a better trailer for my boat. A few months later, I sold my boat and bought a new sofa and chair for our living area. I might go to sleep on the sofa, but I will not drown.

I have learned by making mistakes that preparation is the key to success in anything we do. You cannot teach a good math class without preparing a good lesson plan. You cannot win a football game without preparing a good game plan and preparing your players to execute the game plan. You cannot cook a good meal without preparing and purchasing the right ingredients. You cannot teach a good Sunday School class without research and preparing the lesson. When I taught a large senior adult Sunday

School class for years, I scripted every lesson and rarely deviated from the script.

These are all important, but what is the most important preparation we must make in our lifetime? It is preparation we make to meet our Lord and Savior.

Ezekiel 38:7 says, *Be thou prepared, and prepare for thyself, thou, and all thy company that are assembled unto thee, and be thou a guard unto them.*

1 Peter 1:13 says, *Wherefore gird up the loins of your mind, be sober, and hope to the end for the grace that is to be brought unto you at the revelation of Jesus Christ;*

If we prepare for God, then He will prepare for us as promised in John 14:3. Jesus said, *And if I go and prepare a place for you, I will come again, and receive you unto myself; that where I am, there ye may be also.*

Jack Rogers

Story 36
Parables

In my second book, I have written a devotional story entitled "My Black Book" in which we used humor to relieve the stress of working in junior high school. I wrote that at times we played practical jokes on each other. When our junior high was consolidated with the other junior high school into a new middle school, I later became principal of a large elementary school.

Also in my second book, I have written a devotional story entitled "Friendship and Perseverance" in which I met and became best friends with the new principal of Rome High School. We did a lot of running together and became very close friends.

Unfortunately, we also played practical jokes on each other. For his first year or two, he and his wife still owned a home in the city of Augusta area. One morning I talked our school secretary and our secretary in charge of computer records into calling my friend and pretending to be sheriff deputies and told him that they had caught two families from a different country of origin living in their house. They told him they had run them out of his house, and nothing had been harmed or destroyed.

I knew he was going to pay me back, but I still fell for it anyway. Several months later we had a swing on our playground break while a fifth-grade girl was swinging. Unfortunately, she broke one of her arms. About a week later I received a call from a man pretending to be an attorney representing her family. He said her family was in the process of suing me for negligence in maintaining playground equipment. By that time, I had forgotten my practical joke on my friend, and I fell for it hook, line, and sinker. After that, my friend's wife made us both promise not to play any more practical jokes on each other. Good idea!

We know that in the Bible Jesus was perfect and did not play silly practical jokes on his disciples. He did, however, use parables to illustrate his teachings and to emphasize a point of interest to his disciples.

Jesus provides an answer when asked about his use of parables in the Gospel of Matthew (13: 10 - 17). The disciple came to him and asked, *"Why do you speak to the people in parables?"* He replied, *"The knowledge of the secrets of the Kingdom of Heaven has been given to you, but not to them."*

The parables of Jesus are mostly found in the synoptic gospels. They form approximately one third of his recorded teachings. Christians place great emphasis on these parables, which we generally regard as the words of Jesus.

Many of Jesus's parables refer to simple everyday things, such as a woman baking bread (The parable of the leaven), a man knocking on his neighbor's door at night (the parable of the friend at night), Or the aftermath of a roadside mugging (the parable of the

Jack Rogers

Good Samaritan); Yet they deal with the major religious themes, such as the growth of the Kingdom of God, the importance of prayer, and the meaning of love.

A number of parables which are adjacent, in one or more gospels have similar themes. The parable of the leven follows the parable of the mustard seed in Matthew and Luke, and shares the theme of the Kingdom of Heaven growing from small beginnings. The parable of the hidden treasure and parable of the Pearl form a pair illustrating the great value of the Kingdom of Heaven, and the need for actions in attaining it.

The parables of the lost sheep, lost coin, and lost (prodigal) son Form a trio in Luke dealing with loss and redemption.

The parable of the faithful servant and parable of the ten virgins, adjacent in Matthew, involved waiting for a bridegroom, and have an eschatological theme: Be prepared for the day of reckoning.

Other parables stand alone, such as the parable of the unforgiving servant, dealing with forgiveness; and parable of the Good Samaritan, dealing with practical love; and the parable of the friend at night, dealing with persistence in prayer.

Jesus's parables seem simple, but the messages they convey are deep, and central to his teachings.

Story 37

My way

I think it was Frank Sinatra who first recorded the beautiful song "My Way". I was a teenager in the late 1950s and grew up with Elvis Presley. I like Elvis's version of "My Way" as good or better than that of Frank Sinatra. That may be because I love all of Elvis's songs. I possess several CDs of Elvis's greatest hits including his CD of religious songs. I know it may be sacrilegious to mention Elvis Presley in a devotional story, but after all I am an admitted sinner. I know that he abused prescription drugs, among other things, and did not live a Christian life. He did not live a life that was an example for others to follow, but I did love to hear him sing.

His version of "How Great Thou Art" is one of my favorites. I have spent the last 20 years telling my two sons and daughter-in-law that I want Elvis's version of "How Great Thou Art" played at my memorial. They think I am joking, but I am very serious. Since I will be dead, they probably will not do it, but I plan to haunt them from above or below if they do not follow my direction. I hope you know that I am not serious (maybe).

Getting back to the discussion of the song "My Way". My wife, Sandra, her nurse, Wendy, and I were talking religious matters as we usually do after breakfast and lunch. We are very fortunate that Wendy is a great cook. Wendy commented that what's wrong with the world today is that we want to have it "my way" instead of "God's Way". We have too often adopted the hamburger chain's slogan "Have It Your Way". When we want it "My Way" instead of "God's Way" we have our priorities out of order, and that leads to nothing but trouble. If it is always about me, me, me, we are not following the first commandment *Thou shalt have no other gods before me.*

Thou shalt have no other gods before me means we must put God first in our lives. He is more important than anyone or anything else.

This first commandment sets the tone for the first four commandments. They can be summarized by the great commandment which appears in Deuteronomy 6:5, *And thou shalt love the Lord thy God with all thine heart, and with all thy soul, and with all thy might.*

Jesus set the example of putting God first. In Matthew 4:4 (quoted from Deuteronomy 8: 3), Jesus (even after fasting for 40 days) answered Satan's temptation by saying, *Man shall not live by bread alone, but by every word that proceedeth out of the mouth of God.*

Anything that we put as higher priority than the true God causes us to sin. Doing things "My Way" breaks this command by putting self above God.

Story 38

A son's love for his mother

On this Mother's Day, May 10th, 2020, I felt compelled to share this letter to Wendy Clark, my wife's nurse, from her oldest son, Kadir Kutsal, age 22, which was written a few days earlier on May 6, 2020. I have read similar letters to Wendy from her youngest son Kamran Kutsal, but I chose to share this one from his older brother.

"Don't look at your suffering and struggles in your life as a sad or negative thing. My beautiful mom has taught me that our suffering and struggles through our life refines our faith; It's about hope and strength. I may not see, but I do believe. Jesus wakes my mom up every morning, gives her life, in strength that keeps her strong. She is able to smile and give love to her family, friends, and the whole world in spite of all her many health problems. Every day she experiences nausea and pain from the top of her head to the bottom of her feet. She has a pounding in her chest resulting from a high heart rate, low blood pressure, intestinal bleeding, bleeding in her left kidney, and fluid leaking from the bottom of her brain. She is losing eyesight in her left eye. Her blood vessels and arteries are stretching and getting thinner. To look at her nobody would know what she goes through 24 hours a day, seven days a week.

"If you don't believe in miracles and the power of God, look at my mom's medical records. Look at my mom's smiling face and then examine her medical history again. Then you will understand that God still performs miracles. Our amazing Lord and Savior, Jesus Christ, and his Holy Spirit lives in her. Because of him my beautiful mother glows in the night and day. "

What a profound and loving tribute to a mother from a very loving son. This letter also emphatically shows how Wendy's Christian faith and beliefs have been instilled in her two sons. Proverbs 22:6 says, "Train up a child in the way he should go: and when he is old, he will not depart from it." We should show our children God's love by loving them and others.

Kadir's letter to his mother also follows the directive found in Exodus 20:12 to, *Honour thy father and thy mother: that thy days may be long upon the land which the Lord thy God giveth thee.* Kamran and Kadir are doing that by the lives they live in the love that they have for their mother.

I wish every mother a special "Happy Mother's Day" on this day.

Story 39

Excuses

I am not a computer person. I can check email and send emails. I can receive text messages but cannot send them. I check my Facebook post every day, but I cannot personally post anything on Facebook. I have many excuses for not being a computer person. #1 - I am 77 years old. #2- I have a medical problem with essential tremors in both hands. #3- I have psoriatic arthritis in my hands and cannot make a closed fist in either hand. #4 - My oldest son, Jeff, lives in our same subdivision and can fix any computer problems we have usually within forty-eight hours since he works with computers in his job as a security expert. Lastly, #5- I have a type A personality and refuse to sit in a chair for long periods of time.

All of these are excuses only, because I have always believed we find the time to do the things that are important to us. It is obvious that computers are not a high priority on the list of things I want to do.

On my daily five mile walk this morning I enjoyed the beautiful spring flowers in the neatly landscaped yards in my subdivision. I especially enjoyed the yards with red knockout roses. They were in full bloom and were gorgeous. Even though my lot is very small, it is well landscaped. My backyard is prettier than my front yard. I had several knockout rose bushes in my backyard until one day I discovered a special kind of mole had eaten the roots and destroyed them. They were just lying on the ground. As an excuse, I decided not to replace them because the mole would just come back and destroy them also.

In our religious life we also use all kinds of excuses not to serve our Lord and Savior. #1- I Work so hard I do not have time to worship him. #2- I need to rest and be with my family on Sunday. #3- I am not good enough to be a leader in a church. #4- I see people in the church who are hypocrites. They say one thing in church and do the opposite outside of church.

We can't choose to live a life of sin. If a person finds excuses to sin, that person is not a Christian at all. There are hypocrites everywhere you go. You don't accept Christ for others, you do it for yourself.

There are many examples of people making excuses for not accepting Christ in the Bible: (1) Luke 14: 15-20 *And when one of them that sat at meat with him heard these things, he said unto him, Blessed is he that shall eat bread in the kingdom of God. Then said he unto him, A certain man made a great supper, and bade many: And sent his servant at supper time to say to them that were bidden, Come; for all things are now ready. And they all with one consent began to make excuse. The first said unto him, I have bought a piece of ground, and I must needs go and see it: I pray thee have me excused. And another said, I have bought five yoke of oxen, and I go to prove them: I pray thee have me excused. And another said, I have married a wife, and therefore I cannot come.*

(2) Exodus 4: 10- 14 *but Moses said to the Lord, "O my Lord, I am not eloquent, neither heretofore, nor since thou hast spoken unto thy servant: but I am slow of speech, and of a slow tongue."* ... *"Now therefore go, and I will be with thy mouth, and teach thee what thou shalt say."* But he said, *"O my Lord, send, I pray thee, by the hand of him whom thou wilt send."* ...

(3) Luke 9: 59- 62 to another he said, follow me. But he said *Lord, suffer me first to go and bury my father.* And Jesus said to him, *Let the dead bury their dead: but go thou and preach the kingdom of God.* Yet another said, *I will follow thee; but let me first go bid them farewell, which are at home at my house.* Jesus said to him, *No man, having put his hand to the plough, and looking back, is fit for the kingdom of God.*

We should not be making excuses because they usually lead to sin. One of our founding fathers said, "He that is good for making excuses is seldom good for anything else."

Jack Rogers

Story 40

You Cannot Outrun Yellow Jackets

During the summer while I was in high school and college. I worked several different jobs. A couple of summers I worked for the Alabama Highway Department. For two summers, I worked for an industrial air-conditioning manufacturing plant cutting and fitting pipes. My least favorite summer job was hauling bricks for the construction of a school at Maxwell Air Force Base in Montgomery, Alabama. Of course, all of these were in addition to cutting grass with my two brothers all over the town of Fort Deposit.

When I turned sixteen, my first real job was working with the Alabama Highway Department. We were cutting centerline for the construction of Interstate I-65 between Mobile and Montgomery. At the time, we were working near Georgiana, Alabama.

One day, I was using a bush axe to cut a large brush on the centerline. Little did I know that the brush contained a large nest of yellow jackets. Hundreds of them swarmed toward me and I started running as fast as I could, which was not fast enough. My coach always told me that I had great hands, but slow feet. When I ran marathons, I always finished, but near the back of the pack. After about one-hundred yards, the yellow jackets caught me and I was stung at least twenty times, mostly in the face, neck, and arms. If I had been allergic to yellow jackets, I would have died on the spot. Luckily, I am not allergic, and by taking a couple of aspirins and drinking lots of water, I recovered quickly. My supervisor did let me rest in the van the rest of the day.

I learned that you cannot outrun yellow jackets. In the book of Jonah in the Old Testament, we found out you cannot outrun God.

The book of Jonah was written about 760 B.C., and it is the fifth book in the Minor Prophets. It contains four chapters and forty-eight verses. The author of the books is the prophet Jonah who wrote his own autobiography.

The book opens with God commanding Jonah to go to the city of Nineveh and warn the people to repent or face destruction. Jonah refused because he did not think they deserved to be saved. He tried to flee to the city of Tarshish; he boarded a ship and during the trip, a fierce storm occurred. The experienced sailors were terrified and blamed the storms on Jonah. They eventually threw Jonah into the sea. God had caused the storm to motivate Jonah to be obedient. After the sailors threw Jonah overboard, a great sea mammal swallowed him and eventually spat him onto the seashore after Jonah repented and agreed to obey God. After Jonah preached to the Ninevites they repented. In the final chapter, Jonah is angry because God did not destroy the people. Therefore, since it was very hot, God caused a plant to die and that made Jonah very angry. Then God asked Jonah why he was angry. God used the plant as an illustration. Just as Jonah cared about the plant, God cared about the Ninevites. In the last verse of the book, God reveals that He loved the Ninevites. That is why He wanted the prophet Jonah to rescue them by warning them to repent.

We have learned that we cannot run away from yellow jackets or God. God loves all people and wants all of us to repent and follow him. He controls all things including the sea animals, plants, the wind, and sea. He uses us, his people, to communicate His message to the entire world.

Story 41

Be Kind

Last week after breakfast, my wife, Sandra, her nurse, Wendy, and I were discussing religious topics as we usually do. (By the way, Wendy is an excellent cook and had prepared a delicious omelet for me to enjoy.) Wendy read a statement on her I-phone which I found to be profound. It hit me like a ton of bricks She read "When you have to choose between 'Being Right' and 'Being Kind,' always choose to 'Be Kind.'" The reason it struck me to my core is in the last seventy-seven years, I have always chosen to "Be Right".

I wrote in my first book that I am a very opinionated person. I am a political and religious conservative. I don't apologize for that. My former Superintendent of Schools told me that I see everything black or white (right or wrong). He said there is no gray area with me. He was absolutely correct. I don't argue with people in public, and I have never lost my temper, but people know where I stand and what I believe.

For the last week after Wendy read her statement, I have tried my best to "Be Kind" in every interaction I have. When someone approaches me with a statement I disagree with, I think "Be Kind" and just remain completely silent. After an uncomfortable few seconds, the other person usually changes the subject. Maybe it is not too late to teach an old dog new tricks. We'll see how long it lasts.

Kindness is one of the fruits of the Spirit.

Galatians 5:22-23 says, *But the fruit of the Spirit is love, joy, peace, longsuffering, gentleness, goodness, faith, meekness, temperance: ...*

Ephesians 4:32 says, *And be ye kind one to another, tenderhearted, forgiving one another, even as God for Christ's sake hath forgiven you.*

Proverbs 11:17 says, *The merciful man doeth good to his own soul: but he that is cruel troubleth his own flesh.*

Proverbs 21:21 says, *He that followeth after right-eousness and mercy findeth life, righteousness, and honour.*

Luke 6:31 says, *And as ye would that men should do to you, do ye also to them likewise.*

Some notable quotes are:

"One kind word can change someone's entire day."

"Be somebody who makes everybody feel like a some-body."

"If you want more kindness in the world – put it there."

If "Being Kind" is important enough to be listed as one of the "fruits of the Spirit," then it is important enough for us to live by.

Story 42

Children of God

When my wife, Sandra, and I married in March 1966, I had never been around girls or babies very much. I was the middle of three boys in our family. Sandra was just the opposite. She was the youngest of ten children who were raised on a country farm. There were five girls and five boys. She had been around girls, boys, and babies all her life. While my brother and I were playing football, basketball, and baseball, Sandra was learning how to care for babies and tend to family life.

After we moved to Fitzgerald, Georgia in 1967, we had our first child in October of 1968. Sandra had taken the first semester off from her ninth-grade English teaching position and I was teaching math and coaching football. I took her to the hospital on a Friday afternoon. The doctor assured me that the baby would not come before Saturday afternoon at the earliest, so she told me to go on to the home football game. After the game, I went back to the hospital and the nurse told me to go home and get a good night's sleep because Sandra would need me tomorrow. At 4:00 a.m., my telephone rang and the nurse said to come quickly because the baby was coming. Our baby was born before I arrived at the hospital. The nurse said Sandra and the baby were both fine. At around 8:00 a.m., the nurse brought Jeffrey to our room. Sandra was still on medication and she was talking about the fires in China. The nurse asked me if I wanted to hold him, and I responded yes. Since I had never held a baby before, she showed me how to fold my arms and cradle him. She did not tell me that she was going to leave me alone with our baby for over an hour. I guess she was paying me back for not being there when our baby was born. For over an hour I did not move a muscle. I was scared to death and Sandra was no help since she was still talking about the fires.

I was paid back with our second child because Sandra was in labor for nineteen hours, and I was with her the entire time. After Jason was born, Sandra said that she has had enough of that and had her tubes tied. Two was enough for us. Two great children.

The popular children's song, *Jesus Loves the Little Children* reminds us that all are precious in His sight and no matter your race, gender, or nationality. God wants to see all children come to Him.

Psalms 127:3 says, *Lo, children are an heritage of the Lord: and the fruit of the womb is his reward.*

Matthew 19:14 says, *But Jesus said, Suffer little children, and forbid them not to come unto me, for of such is the kingdom of heaven.*

Proverbs 22:6 says, *Train up a child in the way he should go: and when he is old, he will not depart from it.*

Isaiah 54:13 says, *And all thy children shall be taught of the Lord; and great shall be the peace of thy children.*

Sandra and I consider ourselves the luckiest people on earth to be blessed with two great sons, a great daughter-in-law, and two great granddaughters. They make our lives complete. God has blessed us!

Story 43

It Made it Worthwhile

Just one week ago, on Sunday, May 17, 2020, my daughter-in-law's mother, Martha, passed away after a long battle with Parkinson's disease. She had been in hospice since early February. My wife, Sandra, and I had known Martha for decades. In the 1980s, Sandra and Martha both were English teachers at LaGrange High School in LaGrange, Georgia. When I was named principal at West End Elementary School in Rome, Georgia, Martha was my assistant principal for all seven years before I retired in 2000. She was the one who headed our committee to write our application for "Georgia School of Excellence, "which we won the year before I retired. She also headed the committee to write our application for "Pay for Performance" award, which we won my last year as principal. It sure was nice to receive that $2,000 check which all staff members received that summer.

Martha was the one who arranged the contact between her daughter, Camille, and my oldest son, Jeff, who were both working in Atlanta at the time. They later married in 1994.

Martha died three days after my first book was released on Thursday, May 14th. My daughter-in-law, Camille and her sister, Amelia, and their entire families are spending that long Memorial Day weekend with their father, Gary.

Last night at around 9:00 p.m., I received a telephone call from my oldest granddaughter, Ruth. She said that Martha's husband, Gary, wanted to speak with me. Camille had given him my first book, and he said how much the second story, "Life is not Fair"' meant to him at this time in his mourning over Martha's death. He said it was exactly the thing he needed to read. I told him he not only made my day but made the whole four-month process of getting this book published and printed worth every minute of it.

We never know how much effect one statement, or one conversation can have on another person's life. That is the reason we should be so diligent and guarded in everything that we say and write.

The Bible has a lot to say about how we communicate with others.

James 1:19 *Wherefore, my beloved brethren, let every man be swift to hear, slow to speak, slow to wrath:*

Proverbs 15:1 *A soft answer turneth away wrath: but grievous words stir up anger.*

Ephesians 4:29 *Let no corrupt communication proceed out of your mouth, but that which is good to the use of edifying, that it may minister grace unto the hearers.*

Proverbs 12:18 *There is that speaketh like the piercings of a sword: but the tongue of the wise is health.*

Jack Rogers

James 1:26 *If any man among you seem to be religious, and bridleth not his tongue, but deceiveth his own heart, this man's religion is vain.*

And in closing, I quote Psalms 19:14 *Let the words of my mouth, and the meditation of my heart, be acceptable in thy sight, O Lord, my strength, and my redeemer.*

Story 44

Point of Diminishing Returns

For the last fifteen years my son, Jeff, and I have played in the Bridge Mill Athletic Club Member – Member Golf Tournament. We have enjoyed these times together and have won our flight more than our share of times. We have nice crystal bowls in our trophy cases to keep forever. For the first number of years, I was the better golfer and was able to carry the team. However, in year 2020, I find myself, at age seventy-seven, at a point of diminishing returns. Because of my essential tremors and psoriatic arthritis in both hands, I can no longer compete at a tournament level. Jeff and I played together in our one-day Devil's Triangle Tournament a few weeks ago, and halfway through the tournament I told Jeff to find a new partner for the Member-Member tournament this year. I am no longer able to carry my share of the load. I love golf and do not plan to give it up. Far from it! I am just giving up tournament golf. Our Bridge Mill seniors play every Tuesday and Thursday and I have a nurse, Wendy, to care for my wife on those days.

This is not the first time that I have had to give up something I loved. In my first book, I wrote that I ran three marathons after the age of fifty-five. I was training for my fourth marathon when I developed a rotated pelvis. I cannot even run to the end of my driveway now. However, I have learned to enjoy walking now as an alternative.

I have learned that when we reach a point of diminishing returns in one endeavor, we cannot let ourselves get depressed or down on ourselves. We should look forward to something new that we can get excited about. I realize that I will quickly reach the point of diminishing returns on writing these devotional stories, and when that time comes; I want to find something else that will excite me and motivate me. That is life.

We have all heard that age is just a number, and I do believe that. We can not fall into the trap of believing that at a certain age we can not be productive. I believe what I read in Psalms 92:14 which says, *They will still bear fruit in old age, they will stay fresh and green.*

2 Corinthians 4:16 tells us, *For which cause we faint not; but though our outward man perish, yet the inward man is renewed day by day.*

Isaiah 40:31 says, *But they that wait upon the Lord shall renew their strength; they shall mount up with wings as eagles; they shall run, and not be weary; and they shall walk, and not faint.*

Job 32:7 tells us, *I said, Days should speak, and multitude of years should teach wisdom.*

Ruth 4:15 says, *And he shall be unto thee a restorer of thy life, and a nourisher of thine old age:*

No, we cannot turn back the hands of time, but we can live a more abundant and healthy life right now regardless of how much time has passed or how much we may still have before us. We should change the expression "Point of Diminishing Returns" to "Point of the expectations of the future being as good or better than the past."

About the Author

Jack spent 34 years in education, starting as a math teacher, a football, basketball, baseball coach, and athletic director at a large high school. He was also a boy's Junior High School Assistant Principal, Junior High School Principal, and Elementary School Principal.

He has been married to his wife, Sandra, for 54 years, and they have two sons, Jeff and Jason, and one daughter-in-law, Camille. They have two grand-daughters, Ruth and Rachel.

He has been a member of the Methodist church all of his life. He has served in leadership positions at every level. He has been an elementary Sunday

School teacher, adult teacher, and senior adult teacher.

Jack attended the University of Alabama, Troy University, LaGrange College, Georgia Southern University, and the University of West Georgia. He has a B.A. degree and a master's degree in math and add-on master's degree in Educational Leadership as well as an Educational Specialist (six-year) degree in administration and supervision.

He is a full-time caregiver for his wife, Sandra, who has had Multiple Sclerosis for twenty years and is in a wheelchair. She is a retired English teacher and high school counselor.

Jack's passion is golf, but he loves to exercise. He either plays golf, walks a five-mile trek in the neighborhood, or goes to the fitness center every day but Sunday, when he gives his 77-year-old legs a rest.